THE
MIDLAND

John T. Frederick   *1893 - 1975*

Milton M. Reigelman

THE MIDLAND

A Venture in Literary Regionalism

UNIVERSITY OF IOWA PRESS • IOWA CITY

Library of Congress Cataloging in Publication Data

Reigelman, Milton M   1942-
   The Midland.

   Bibliography: p.
   Includes indexes.
   1. The Midland.   2.   Regionalism in literature.
I. Title.
PS563.M4R4   810'.5   75-28219
ISBN 0-87745-054-4

PS
563
my
R4

University of Iowa Press, Iowa City 52242
© 1975 by The University of Iowa
All rights reserved
Printed in the United States of America

To Sandy

Contents

Preface   ix

Introduction   xi

I: THE HISTORY   1

    Beginnings: 1915-1919   1
    The Net of Associate Editors   7
    The "Glennie" Frontier: 1919-1921   11
    Return to Iowa: 1921-1930   15
    H. L. Mencken and Frank Luther Mott   19
    Midland and the Young Writer   23
    An "Uncommercial Magazine with an
       Impecunious Publisher"   27
    Midland in Chicago: 1930-1933   31

II: THE EDITORIAL POLICY — REGIONALISM   41

    New York: The Blind Giant   42
    Rural Stereotypes and Eastern Plots   45
    Anti-Local Color, Anti-Gentility, Anti-Romance   50
    The Use of the Past   53
    Experimentalism and the New Psychology   57
    Midland's Assessment of American Literature:
       The Past, The Southerners, and The Negroes   60
    The Midwestern Novelists of the Twenties   64
    The Poets and Neihardt   66
    Midland's Regionalism in Retrospect   70

III: THE LITERATURE   75

    The Pervasive Family   76
    The Old vs. the Young   81
    The City Story and the Country Story   84
    Stories of the "Great War"   89
    Midland Social Realism   91
    Raymond Weeks and "Folk Humor"   93
    Midland Poetry   95
    Midland's Literature in Perspective   100

Appendix I: Index of Contributors, 1915-1933   103

Appendix II: Index to *Midland* Book Reviews   117

Bibliography   133

Preface

WHEN I first became interested in *The Midland* in 1967, there were only nineteen files of the magazine extant. Therefore, one of my first debts is to the Kraus Reprint Company which, that year, reprinted 500 copies of the magazine, ending its scarcity.

This book would not have been possible without the sympathetic cooperation of octogenarian John T. Frederick. Despite frequent ill health over the past few years, Frederick has been willing to talk with me for long hours about *Midland,* to direct me to other sources of information, and to respond promptly to written inquiries after I left Iowa, where Frederick resides.

Some early *Midland* correspondence was destroyed in Chicago when Frederick's basement flooded in 1935. But other correspondence from the period has survived, and this study draws from several hundred letters between Frederick and other editors or authors which have not heretofore been generally available. I am grateful to Mrs. Mildred Mott Wedel, Frank Luther Mott's daughter, who helped me recover some of this correspondence and other manuscript items by spending a day of her Christmas holidays in her basement going through some of her father's papers with me. Librarians at the following libraries also aided in this recovery effort: the university libraries at Chicago, Iowa, Missouri, Montana, Nebraska, Notre Dame, Vanderbilt, and Wisconsin; the Iowa and Wisconsin State Historical Societies; the Newberry Library; and the New York Public Library.

Also most helpful were letters I received—some containing correspondence and other materials from the 1915-1933 period—from the following *Midland* contributors and friends: Charles Allen, Clarence Andrews, Benjamin Appel, John Beadle, Richard W. Borst, Irving Brant, Sargent Bush, Jr., Marquis W. Childs, Paul Corey, August Derleth, Babette Deutsch, Thomas Duncan, Loren C. Eiseley, James T. Farrell, Marie E. Gilchrist, Albert Halper, Margaret Hartley, Harry Hartwick, James Hearst, Jay B. Hubbell, Howard Mumford Jones, MacKinlay Kantor, Max L. Marshall, Harold G. Merriam, Clarice Muilenburg, James Muilenburg, John G. Neihardt, Henry Nash Smith, and Paul R. Stewart.

I wish to thank Delight Ansley, Alma Hovey, Bruce Mahan, Baldwin

Maxwell, and Warren Van Dine; in one or more interviews, each was helpful in reconstructing a part of the journal's history.

I am also grateful to the following people for offering helpful advice, criticism, and encouragement in the early stages of this study: Paul Engle, John C. Gerber, William Hagen, W. R. Irwin, Leslie Moeller, Sherman Paul, and Michael Sewell. Special thanks go to Paul Baender for reading the manuscript critically in some of its various stages of imperfection.

Four of my colleagues—Paul Cantrell, Charles T. Hazelrigg, Mary Sweeney, and Roberta H. White—graciously suggested stylistic changes in parts of the manuscript; the infelicities are, of course, my own. I am indebted to the Centre College Committee on Faculty Research for granting me a stipend during the summer of 1973, making it possible to complete the research for the book. And it gives me special pleasure to thank Ethel F. Reigelman for various help during the study, because she is my mother.

The most crucial debt is to the person who, from the inception of this project, has been of more help to me and to the project than she knows, and to whom the book is dedicated.

Introduction

In 1930 the monthly review of literature, *The Bookman*, took a retrospective look at a most curious phenomenon in American literary history: the rise of the "little magazines." Beginning about 1912 as the lonely gesture of a few discontented individuals, the article stated, the little magazines quickly became the ordinary mode of communication in America for literary challenge and reform; "from every province of the literary empire, fresh recruits enlisted in the motley army that marched with such arrogant confidence against the trembling *ancien regime*."[1] A curious rabble these little magazines certainly were with their often eccentric dress, their unorthodox tastes, and their erratic temperaments. Yet for the second fifteen years of the twentieth century they served as the advance guard of American literature, the rear guard being the commercial publishers who simply would not accept a writer until the advance guard had proven his worth and his potential salability.

It was partly because the economics of publishing a magazine in America had changed so drastically around the turn of the century that the little magazines were born. During the 1890s the publishers of the major journals discovered what Theodore Peterson has called a "basic economic principle of twentieth-century magazine publishing":

> one could achieve a large circulation by selling his magazine for much less than its cost of production and could take his profits from the high volume of advertising that a large circulation attracted.[2]

Several major publishers slashed their subscription rates and greatly expanded their circulation, with the result that by the early twentieth century almost all magazines were forced to appeal to wider audiences in order to remain economically viable. Malcolm Cowley has pointed out that shortly after 1910 even the prestigious *Atlantic Monthly*, which had published some of the best nineteenth-century American literature, "surrendered some of its literary standing" in order to appeal to more readers. As the gulf between "the tastes of the broad public and the aims of serious writers"[3] became more apparent, little magazines began to spring up.

Between 1910 and 1920 eighty-four little magazines were founded, and that number doubled in the twenties. Most were short-lived. That they were immensely important for the development of American literature is clear from the fact that they discovered and encouraged such writers as T. S. Eliot, Wallace Stevens, Sherwood Anderson, Ernest Hemingway, Carl Sandburg, and William Faulkner – by one accounting made in 1943, more than three-fourths of the important post-1912 poets, novelists, and critics. [4]

Literary historians generally use 1912, the year Harriet Monroe founded *Poetry* in Chicago, as the beginning of the movement and 1930, when the Depression began taking its toll, as its end. *Poetry* and a few others survived the thirties. Indeed, we still have what might be called "little magazines" with us in the seventies, although most of them are subsidized by foundations or universities and are both less exciting and less influential than their ancestors.

Probably the best definition of a little magazine is that of Frederick J. Hoffman, Charles Allen, and Carolyn F. Ulrich in *The Little Magazine: A History and a Bibliography,* first published by Princeton University Press in 1946, but still an authoritative history of the movement. They described a little magazine as one "designed to print artistic work which for reasons of commercial expedience is not acceptable to the money-minded periodicals or presses." The "little" refers primarily to the size of the audience, but also reflects a conscious opposition to the standards of the "big" magazines. (The same is true for the "little theatre" movement in America, which also got its start in the teens.)

Some of the best-known little magazines of the twenties, like Margaret Anderson's unpredictable *The Little Review,* got their start in Chicago, the center of the midwestern literary awakening. This study is about *The Midland,* a magazine lesser known than *The Little Review,* but in some ways no less important. From 1915 until 1933, *Midland* was the abiding passion of John T. Frederick, an Iowan who was its editor throughout. As Frederick moved around the Midwest, so did his magazine – from Iowa, to Minnesota, to Michigan, back to Iowa, and finally to Chicago. During the late twenties, when Frederick and *Midland* were back in Iowa, the magazine was coedited by Frank Luther Mott, later the longtime dean of the University of Missouri School of Journalism, and the author of the definitive, five-volume, *A History of American Magazines.*

Over the years there has been general agreement that *Midland* occupies a special place in American literary history. In 1923, H. L. Mencken called *Midland* "probably the most influential literary periodical ever set up in America." [5] In 1946, the authors of *The Little Magazine* stated that *Midland* "must be ranked alongside" Emerson's nineteenth-century forum for the transcendental movement, *The Dial;* the magazine which serialized Joyce's *Ulysses* from 1918-1921, *The Little Review;* and the most important of all the little magazines, *Poetry.*[6] More recently John Tebbel in *The American Magazine: A Compact History* has written:

> Regional publishing of little magazines was particularly important to the developing literary culture of this century because it enabled the Midwest, particularly, to break away from the eastern dominance and give its new writers a show case, while to the Southwest and in the Far West it meant an opportunity for publication virtually denied to the writers of those regions. The best of the regional periodicals may have been John T. Frederick's *Midland. . . .*[7]

Because it was a basic principle of *Midland* never to pay for contributions, established major writers who could command large sums for their work in the commercial magazines did not publish there. One does find in its pages, however, the work of many important regional writers and the beginning work of others who were to become prominent critics, playwrights, journalists, and naturalists: James T. Farrell, MacKinlay Kantor, Ruth Suckow, William March, Cleanth Brooks, Howard Mumford Jones, Mark Van Doren, Louis Kronenberger, John G. Neihardt, Babette Deutsch, Paul Engle, Maxwell Anderson, Marquis Childs, Loren Eiseley.

Part I of this study traces the history of *Midland,* which is of special interest because, as Reed Whittemore has recently written, "the dimensions of Frederick's enterprise . . . and the informal, amateur spirit in which it was conducted make it an extremely pure example of the little magazine act." [8] In its difficulties and in its successes, *Midland* was typical of scores of struggling little magazines of the late teens and twenties. Its whole editorial operation became, in fact, a kind of model for many regional magazines that followed in its wake. To understand its rise from a small, local undertaking in 1915 to a position of some national prominence in 1933 is to understand a small but colorful piece of American literary history.

Part II focuses on the magazine's editorial pages. Literary historians have often stated that twentieth-century regionalism was first enunciated in the editorial policy of *Midland.*[9] Precisely what twentieth-century regionalism is, however, has not been clear. The authors of *The Little Magazine* spoke of the "immense volume of violent controversy, in print and out of print" over regional literature. Its defenders and detractors, they said, have "piled high a mass of misinformation, wild opinion, deliberate falsification, slanderous bad temper; and the critical confusion that has resulted will not be unscrambled for a long time."[10] Here we shall attempt to end some of this confusion.

Part III briefly surveys and assesses the more than 1,000 poems and 400 short stories *Midland* published during its eighteen years of existence. *Midland* authors were learning that the first requirement of a writer is that he write honestly and sensitively—without an eye to salability—about what he knows best. The world these authors portray is perhaps of special interest to us today because it is so markedly different from the postwar, wasteland world portrayed in much of the better-known fiction of the 1920s.

The appendices contain indexes designed to make *Midland* more usable for the scholar and more accessible to the reader with an interest in the period. Appendix 1 is a single index of all literature *Midland* printed. Yearly indexes were provided to libraries receiving the magazine, but those indexes were neither cumulative, consistent, nor even always accurate. [11] Appendix 2 indexes each of the more than 500 authors treated in *Midland* book reviews and essays.

NOTES

1   William Troy, "The Story of the Little Magazines: Making No Compromise with the Public Taste," *The Bookman* 70 (February 1930):657.
2   *Magazines in the Twentieth Century* (Urbana, 1964), p. 7.
3   "Magazine Business, 1910-1946," *New Republic* 115 (21 October 1946):521. *Atlantic Monthly,* founded in 1857, was edited by James Russell Lowell, and later by William Dean Howells. Howells once listed the following as the most significant *Atlantic* contributors before his time: Longfellow, Emerson, Hawthorne, Whittier, Holmes, Lowell, Harriet Beecher Stowe, and Bryant.
4   Charles Allen, "The Advance Guard," *The Sewanee Review* 51 (July/September 1943):425-29.
5   *The Smart Set* (July 1923):141.
6   Frederick J. Hoffman, Charles Allen, and Carolyn F. Ulrich, *The Little Magazine: A History and A Bibliography* (Princeton, 1946), p. 147.
7   *The American Magazine: A Compact History* (New York, 1969), p. 9.
8   Reed Whittemore, *Little Magazines* (Minneapolis, 1963), p. 40.
9   The following comment is typical:
"As we have said, literary regionalism was given its first conscious statement in *The Midland* and the little magazines that followed it."
The Little Magazine, p. 133.
10   *The Little Magazine,* p. 128.
11   The eighteen individual indexes were never compiled, probably at least partly because they are not consistent. Some indexes list only authors of fiction while others list authors of fiction and editorials, as well as titles of works. Moreover the individual indexes contain wrong page numbers (e.g., although the index to XIV lists Henry L. Wilson's story on 195, it is on 125), errors in names (e.g., the index to XIV lists Richard Elpers as Ruth Elpers), and minor and major omissions (e.g., the index to IV leaves out L. H. Bailey's essay on 103; the index to XI does not include the six authors whose work appears in the November issue).

The MIDLAND
A Venture in Literary Regionalism

THE story of *Midland* is in large part the story of one man, John T. Frederick, for during the whole life of the magazine the two were inseparable. During 1913 and 1914, while Frederick was still an undergraduate at the University of Iowa, he discussed the idea of a midwestern literary magazine with other Iowans and midwesterners and began planning for its first issue. From 1915 until 1933 he edited *Midland,* published it, wrote for it, defended it, lectured endlessly about it, used it in his college classes, and mailed out its copies. In the 1930s he seriously jeopardized the well-being of his family by accruing a huge personal debt for it. When it finally succumbed to the Depression in 1933, he wrote its epitaph.

One wonders what could have caused Frederick, who was twenty-one years old in 1915, not only to begin such an undertaking but also to sustain it for the next eighteen and one-half years. Frederick J. Hoffman, the foremost authority of the little-magazine movement, wrote that little-magazine editors as diverse as William Carlos Williams, Ezra Pound, and Norman Macleod were all driven by "some form of discontent." [1] They viewed the official, commercial publishers of their time "with disdain, sometimes with despair," he said. John T. Frederick was discontented from the beginning with the dominance of the New York-based magazines and publishing houses. His journal was conceived as—and remained throughout its existence—a challenge to that dominance.

Frederick himself put it best in an editorial. He wrote that in 1915, because there was no general literary magazine of high quality "published between the Alleghenies and the Rockies," young midwestern writers were more or less being forced to go East and meet publishing standards which did not allow them to treat their region realistically and honestly: "A result has seemed to be a tendency to false emphasis, distortion, in literary interpretations."[2] By establishing a noncommercial magazine sympathetic to midwestern interest, Frederick hoped to make it easier for young writers to stay in their native region and avoid the debilitating influence of New York. If they could be encouraged to remain in the Middle West, he thought, both the writers and the region would profit. This notion, fundamental to *Midland*'s editorial policy, was articulated on page one of the journal's first issue:

> Possibly the region between the mountains would gain in variety at least if it retained more of its makers of literature, music, pictures, and other expressions of civilization. And possibly civilization itself might be with us a somewhat swifter process if expression of its spirit were more frequent. Scotland is none the worse for Burns and Scott, none the worse that they did not move to London and interpret London themes for London publishers. (1.1)

In some ways Frederick was an unlikely person to have mounted such a challenge. When he began publishing, he was still an undergraduate without either personal wealth or significant financial backing. But his background had prepared him well to edit a magazine that would be devoted primarily to authentic literature of the small-town and rural Midwest.

He was born in 1893 near Corning, Iowa, in the less prosperous south-western part of the state.[3] His paternal grandfather, a first-generation American, had migrated to Adams County, Iowa, before the Civil War from a German settlement in southeastern Pennsylvania; his maternal grandparents had migrated to Iowa from New York state, where their families had lived since Colonial times. Although most of Frederick's time as a boy was taken up working on his father's small, hilly farm, he also found time to read. There were many religious books in his home — his maternal grandfather had been a minister — and also a sprinkling of good fiction: the first book he remembers reading was *Huckleberry Finn*. Perhaps the most important person in his boyhood was his mother's only brother, Judge Horace M. Towner, who lived nearby and was later elected U.S. congressman and appointed governor of Puerto Rico. Judge Towner often read aloud to his nephew, saw to it that Frederick was tutored in both Greek and German (by the Congregational minister and a high school teacher), and helped steer him toward the University of Iowa at Iowa City, where the judge was a part-time member of the law faculty.

Frederick entered the University in 1909, when he was sixteen, but had to leave after his sophomore year for financial reasons. For the next two years he lived in Prescott, Iowa, a rural village of four hundred people. There he was high school principal, athletic coach, and sole high school teacher. By the time he returned to the University in 1913, he had developed a special interest in contemporary American literature; once at the University, he quickly distinguished himself by what a fellow student has called his "critical brilliance." [4]   He debated, was elected to Phi Beta Kappa, was voted president of the senior class, and was chosen as head of a small group of student and faculty writers called the Athelney Club.

It was in the Athelney Club in 1913 that the idea of publishing a regional literary magazine was first discussed. No one remembers who actually first brought up the idea, but it might well have been the man whom Frederick later credited with having the inspiration for the magazine: C. F. (Clarke Fisher) Ansley.

Ansley was one of those little-known figures who work largely behind the scenes, but whose ideas influence others and bear rich fruit. He was, among other things, probably the first person to envision the University of Iowa as a center for creative writing. When Frederick first met him at the University in 1911, he was well established there as chairman of the English department and dean of the College of Fine Arts. Yet he was already beginning to have serious differences with some members of the University administration. For Ansley was a strong advocate of "the higher provincialism," a term which the Harvard philosopher Josiah Royce had used in his Phi Beta Kappa address on "Provincialism" that Ansley had heard him deliver in Iowa City in 1902. In that speech Royce had stated that the forces of industrialism were turning Americans into near automatons. To prevent this from happening, Royce argued, regions with distinct cultural patterns should encourage their individualities and promote a "higher provincialism":

> Let your province then be your first social idea. Cultivate its young men, and keep them near you. Foster provincial independence. Adorn your surroundings with beauty of art. Serve faithfully your community that the nation may be served. [5]

Ansley was precisely the kind of person Royce must have hoped to reach in his address. He was not only an impressive Old English scholar and teacher (he had done graduate work at the Universities of Leipzig, Heidelberg, and Paris and had gone from instructor to full professor in six years); he also had a deep understanding and appreciation of his midwestern heritage. [6] As a boy, he had been a page in the Illinois legislature where his father, a country doctor, served. Both father and son undoubtedly knew men in Springfield who had earlier worked with Abraham Lincoln. As an undergraduate at the University of Nebraska, Ansley had married a girl whose father, an army surgeon, had lived for years among the Pawnee Indians.

Ansley's differences with some administrators at the University of Iowa had to do with his insistence that the creative efforts of students and teachers in his English department counted as heavily as their scholarly efforts. Frederick later said that Ansley expected his students to learn about the culture of the Anglo-Saxons, but also to learn about the culture of their own American Midwest. Partly toward this latter end, Ansley organized an extracurricular "Readers' Club" in which contemporary American as well as older selections of literature were orally interpreted by the members. Then in 1911 he helped to found Athelney, a select group of students and faculty who read, discussed, and criticized their own writing frequently at his commodious Victorian home (still standing at 902 Iowa Avenue). The club was named for the small island off the coast of England where King Alfred took refuge from the onslaught of Danes in 878. The foreword to Athelney's 1914 literary anthology, written by Ansley, suggests that the eleven student and faculty members thought of themselves as doing on a small scale what *Midland* would soon attempt on a large scale:

> That name [Athelney] reminds us of Alfred the Great, 'soothfast and steadfast,' who saved to the world what Anglo-Saxon speech and literature and government and Christianity have meant and will mean. He had to fight the heathen, sometimes 'with a little band'; but as often as victory gave him 'stillness,' he used it joyously in collecting and enriching our literature. [7]

When this foreword was published, Frederick was a tall, spare junior. Like Ansley, he was convinced that the time was ripe for a literary magazine that would tap and develop regional writing from the Midwest. During the spring of 1914, when Frederick began planning for the magazine, Ansley was of particular help in soliciting material and support from writers he knew throughout the region. By nature, Frederick was cautious. The rationale for the journal and for much of its editorial policy was clear to him by late spring, but he did not want to begin publishing until he had enough subscribers and manuscripts to assure the journal's success for at least a year. The scheduled publication date of the first issue, originally October 1914, was delayed. By the end of the year when 190 people had sent in $1.50 and Frederick had—in hand or promised—enough material for twelve issues, he was finally ready to begin.

Frederick had earlier decided to name the magazine *The Midland: A Magazine of the Middle West,* partly in recognition of *The Midland Monthly,* a magazine published in Des Moines, Iowa, from 1894-99. The earlier magazine had a general rather than a literary orientation, featuring articles on travel, history, and education along with some fiction. It was a fairly large, commercial operation, but it did have a regional cast, and its editor, Johnson Brigham, later the state librarian, would have agreed with a statement in a prepublication flyer for Frederick's magazine:

> The general interests of the Middle West will receive proper attention only in the pages of a Middle Western magazine.[8]

Midland's first issue appeared on 6 January 1915; it was an event that went largely unnoticed outside Iowa City. Each of the three Iowa City newspapers, however, noted the event enthusiastically, insuring the magazine at least a warm local reception. The *Iowa City Daily Press* announced *Midland*'s birth in a review which appeared under the headline "The Midland Appears Today" and the subhead "Iowa and Middle West Represented by a Real Magizine [*sic*], Published Here":

> 'The Midland' made its bow to the public that reads and thinks, today.
> Vol. 1, No. 1, of this distinctively western magazine made its appearance on the Press' reviewing table, this morning, and was as welcome as the new year. . . .
>
> The introductory literary riches on the well-laden table with which the Midland provides its guests a real feast, indicate that the longevity of the magazine ougth [*sic*] to be as great as it will be welcome. . . .
> Because, in Iowa and the Middle West, instead of New York and the east, the Midland's contributors, present and future, reside, these gifted men and women will be none the worse. . . .
>
> To the Midland, deserving much; and to its earnest and capable projectors, the people of Iowa and the Midwest will invoke success and that measure of prosperity which magazine and men abundantly merit.[9]

If that first *Midland* critic saw in the magazine glimmerings of permanence, it was no doubt partly because the item laid on his reviewing table *looked* so distinctive. Some little magazines of the era, like Yvor Winters's *Gyroscope*, were mimeographed. But *Midland* was a painstakingly designed, carefully made magazine with watermarked, deckle-edged octavo pages bound in an attractive tan cover. John Springer, an ex-legislator, book collector, and master printer in what Frederick called "the finest old tradition of the craft,"[10] was responsible for the magazine's initial design and for maintaining its printed quality. Even though Frederick was to move around frequently, throughout *Midland*'s existence it was always printed under Springer's direction in the Economy Advertising Company, an Iowa City printing firm still in existence.

Frederick's appreciation of quality design and printing had editorial implications for *Midland*, since both he and his coeditor in the late twenties, Frank Luther Mott, interpreted the standard design and cheap production magazines and books coming from most of the bigger presses as yet another sign of the movement toward commercialization and mass culture. In reviews Mott often gave special praise to books that were well-made in addition to being well-written. In reviewing a biography of Washington Irving, he began as follows:

> Here is a lovely piece of work. To begin with, the book is beautifully made, so that one begins to like it before one reads a line. Leigh Hunt relates an extreme instance when he tells of seeing Lamb 'give a kiss to an old folio,' but why not? Beautiful books inspire lasting affection. (12.198)

And in an editorial essay Frederick, who once served as apprentice to Springer, wrote that he cherished the ambition of someday printing with his own hands some of the works of William Morris, Walt Whitman, Bertrand Russell, and other of his favorite writers:

> The editor finds much pleasure in the thought of putting into type the words and sentences of these books, and printing the pages: with time enough to taste the phrase and sound the thought, or look out at the grouse in the poplar trees. Meanwhile . . . the editor can at least read them when he will; and although the pages which he reads show too plainly the mark of the machine and too little the love of the workman, he cannot but give thanks for them to all living and dead masters of the great craft in which he is the most humble of apprentices. (7.63-64)

Midland's first issue contained only one essay, one short story, and one poem, but each was by a midwesterner relatively well known at the time. The essay was by the Iowa writer James B. Weaver, whose father, General James B. Weaver, had captured twenty-two electoral votes for president of the United States as the Populist candidate in 1892. The short story was by Keene Abbott, a writer and critic for the *Omaha World-Herald* and author of numerous stories of American Indian life. And the poem was by Arthur Davison Ficke, a Davenport, Iowa, poet who had by then published several volumes of verse and was regularly appearing in *Poetry*. During the first year of publication many of the contributors—such as Hartley Alexander, a professor of philosophy at the University of Nebraska—taught at midwestern schools; others— such as Irving Brant, chief editorial writer of the *St. Louis Star*—were in journalism. Most of the early essays and articles had a specifically midwestern appeal, such as "Autumn on the Upper Mississippi," and "Amana the Church and Christian Metz the Prophet."

There were two special departments. "The Midland Chronicle," which only lasted one year, called attention to midwestern art exhibits, meetings, and journals such as the newly established *Mississippi Valley Historical Review.* "The Midland Library" contained a series of short, unsigned reviews of books by authors from the region. From the beginning, the short reviews in this section were supplemented by longer, signed reviews which appeared separately.

During 1915, about a third of the magazine's space was taken up with essays and articles, a third with fiction, and a third with poetry. After four or five issues, Frederick started receiving many more manuscripts—especially stories—than he ever expected from young, unestablished writers. In order to give more space to their work he began reducing the space given to essays and poetry. By 1918 the equal mix of nonfiction, fiction, and poetry had given way to what became the pattern for the rest of *Midland*'s years: mostly fiction with some poetry. When the magazine ceased publication in 1933, Harriet Monroe told her *Poetry* audience something that had become increasingly true. She said that while *Midland* had always published admirable verse, "it has been distinguished chiefly by the excellence and originality of its choice of prose." [11]

The Net of Associate Editors

DURING the first year, the magazine listed an array of staff positions including editor, managing editor, associate editor, literary editor, department editor, and consulting editor. This setup changed quickly. Frederick soon found that the division of duties traditional for the larger, established magazines was simply not practical for *Midland,* which was essentially a one-man magazine. After that first year the staff box listed only Frederick as "Editor, Publisher, and Owner," plus a group of "Associate Editors." [12] Usually there were ten, all of whom occasionally advised Frederick on particular manuscripts. Because these associates moved throughout the Midwest, and many taught at large universities, they formed a kind of shifting net which covered key spots in the search for new talent.

Probably the most important of the associate editors (besides C. F. Ansley) was Professor Edwin Ford Piper, a stocky bachelor who was one of the Athelney faculty members. Piper taught courses in Chaucer at Iowa, wrote poetry about the Nebraska frontier of his boyhood, and was an early collector of midwestern ballads.[13] Perennially, he offered an informal, Saturday morning, non-credit writing "class" composed of a few students who would criticize one another's poetry under his guidance. Frederick was a member of this class and for the first few issues of the magazine relied heavily on Piper's judgment regarding poetry. Piper, an enthusiastic backer of *Midland* from its inception, was one of twelve people who donated twenty-five dollars to the magazine in 1914 so that "the magazine shall be secured against insolvency."[14]

Of the associate editors, Piper was the only one who lived in Iowa City throughout *Midland's* existence. Ansley moved to Michigan, then to Nebraska, then to the East. Two classmates of Frederick who were associate editors left Iowa City after completing their master's degrees: Ival McPeak went to Minneapolis to teach; Roger Sergel went to Pittsburgh to teach and then to Chicago, where he became a publisher.

Esther Paulus, another associate editor, had grown up on a third-generation Iowa farm five miles east of Iowa City.[15] At the University she was one of the two female members of Athelney and helped with *Midland* during its first year. She then made her relationship with the magazine permanent by marrying Frederick. A literary historian would call it an ideal marriage, for she was independent and competent, so that later Frederick could leave her in charge of both the magazine and their two sons and take month-long trips on behalf of *Midland.* She had a fine critical sense to match her husband's, and could often help him in reviewing manuscripts. Most importantly, she believed enough in *Midland* to make enormous personal and financial sacrifices to keep it going during the next seventeen years.

Four other associate editors were strategically spread out in key university towns from the beginning: Roy Tower in Bloomington, Indiana; Mary Grove Chawner in Evanston, Illinois; Nelson A. Crawford in Manhattan, Kansas; and Hartley Alexander in Lincoln, Nebraska.

While Frederick remained in Iowa City, putting out the magazine was a fairly simple operation. With occasional advice from others he decided what should be published, gave the manuscripts to John Springer, later read the proofs, and then picked up the magazines for mailing. The clerical work was done by Frederick himself, or by his wife. When Frederick moved away from Iowa City in 1917, the operation became more time-consuming. Even though there were associate editors in Iowa City who might have done it for him, Frederick wanted to work with Springer on layout and to read the proofs himself; everything had to be mailed back and forth. Later still, when Frederick began lecture tours, the logistics of putting out the magazine became even more complicated. Manuscripts mailed to him at designated points along his route were missed; subscriptions he received while on the road were lost; communication between him and Springer was more difficult; and the magazine was sometimes embarrassingly late in coming out. There was always an informality about *Midland* business operations that was perhaps in keeping with the amateur spirit of the magazine. Often, as the following letters [16] suggest, subscribers and contributors were much inconvenienced:

> I am wondering just what it does take to be a subscriber. Last summer I wrote you how much I liked the new number and sent two years' subscription. That seemed to be enough to put me off the list forever. My magazine stopped coming at once. I am wondering now just how to get on the list again. Will I have to wait until the second year expires and *then* write you that I think you publish a bum magazine and I'm never going to take it again?
>
> (Letter from a subscriber to Frederick)

> When I received your letter of inquiry of just a month ago, I wrote to an associate editor in Iowa City who had charge of the forwarding of manuscripts this spring and summer while I was lecturing, and later, was at Glennie. He opened the mss. which came to Iowa City, forwarding some and returning others — and keeping still others, it seems, inadvertently but none the less surely. I am equally to blame in the matter, no doubt, for I remember receiving early in July a letter from you stating that you had received no action on the earlier group you had sent. . . .
>
> (Letter from Frederick to a contributor)

Dear friend:
   The first issues of *The Midland* for 1920 have been unavoidably delayed for many weeks. They will be ready for mailing very soon, and beginning with April regularity seems possible. I appreciate your patience.
>
> (Printed postcard from Frederick to subscribers)

The first issue for 1920 finally did reach the subscribers in July of that year. [17] Yet in spite of this and other inconveniences, enough people kept renewing their subscriptions to keep *Midland* publishing. This was no doubt partly because they were such an elite group. For much of *Midland*'s history, its subscribers numbered less than five hundred, a very select few compared, for example, to the two and one-quarter million people who subscribed to *McCall's* at the time. Frederick was able to correspond with many of his subscribers personally, and he frequently asked for their opinions and their help in the pages of the magazine. Although he admitted that the editors never consciously considered readers' tastes in accepting or rejecting manuscripts ("We try, quite frankly, to please ourselves. What we like best we print" [18.204].), he added that subscribers still played a real part in the work of *Midland,* which was encouraging promising new writers:

> This does not mean, however, that we are not interested in the reactions of readers. We value comments on our choices, adverse opinions as well as those which are favorable both for our contributors and for ourselves. Oftentimes a reader's comment means a great deal to a writer, especially a young writer whose work is appearing for the first time, as is so often the case with contributors to *The Midland.* We always try to pass on such comments, and we appreciate almost as much as do the writers the occasional personal letters of comments, addressed to contributors, which pass through our hands. But also our job as editors becomes increasingly fascinating when we have concrete evidence of our readers' participation in, and of their pleasure or disappointment in our results.

In 1917 Frederick finished his master's thesis at the University of Iowa. Through the efforts of an exclassmate who had gone earlier to teach at the State Normal College at Moorhead, Minnesota, Frederick was offered the chairmanship of the small English department there. Thinking that *Midland* was healthy enough to survive outside the environment that nurtured it, he took the job.

One reason he thought the magazine could withstand the move was that it had been acclaimed by Edward J. O'Brien, the influential critic, author, and editor of the annual *Best Short Stories* volumes from 1914 to 1940. In O'Brien's anthology for 1915, he had classified every story *Midland* published during its first year as "distinctive," and had singled out the fledgling magazine for soaring praise:

> One new periodical . . . claims unique attention this year for . . . recent achievement and abundant future promise. A year ago a slender little monthly magazine entitled the *Midland* was first issued in Iowa City. It attracted very little attention, and in the course of the year published but ten short stories. It has been my pleasure and wonder to find in these ten stories the most vital interpretation in fiction of our national life that many years have been able to show. Since the most brilliant days of the

New England men of letters, no such white hope has proclaimed itself with such assurance and modesty.

In his anthology for 1916, O'Brien credited the new magazine with helping to prepare the way for the group of Chicago writers who had just burst onto the literary scene.

It is no mere coincidence that the finest expression of our national life among the younger men is coming out of the Middle West. *The Midland* has been a fruitful influence, and out of Chicago have come a band of writers including Anderson, Buzzell, Hecht, Lindsay, Masters, and Sandburg with an altogether new substance, saturated with the truth of the life they have experienced.[18]

After these remarks, other national recognition was not long in coming. *Current Opinion* began reprinting poems and stories originally published in *Midland* and prefacing the pieces with comments like the following:

The Midland, 'a magazine of the Middle West,'... publishes real literature (as we have had occasion to say before) and it is literature drawn out of the life of America's plain people.[19]

Magazines like *The New Republic* began talking about *Midland* as a part of the American literary renaissance that *Poetry* had originally encouraged:

Neither the Little Review nor the Midland publishes poetry alone, but each makes a distinctive contribution to the renaissance. The Midland specializes in quiet. Did Robert Frost write about the middle west he would be its ideal contributor. As it is, Edwin Ford Piper, using Frost's technique, pours his whole output into this friendly medium, and sets a restful tone.[20]

In short, by the end of 1919, after a local but enthusiastic welcome into the world, a childhood nurtured by favorable critical comment, and a move away from home, *Midland* was solidly enough established to begin the twenties as a regional magazine of some national repute.

The "Glennie" Frontier: 1919-1921

MOST regional movements during the twenties and thirties were characterized by ruralism; the Southern Agrarians, for example, preached that life in the cities was "particularly debased."[21] In the spring of 1919 *Midland* became rural in more than its editorial pronouncements.

Frederick resigned his job in Minnesota, and moved himself, his family, and his magazine to a wilderness area on the northern end of Michigan's lower peninsula where pioneer conditions prevailed.

Several years earlier real estate speculators had interested a group of Iowa professors in investing in land in this cut-over pine country near Glennie, Michigan. Among those who invested, C. F. Ansley was probably the most optimistic about his purchase. Each summer he took his family there where they began building a cabin on their immense tract of land, which was a half-day's drive from the nearest store. Ansley's daughter, Delight Ansley, recalls that only one other white man lived in the township, and that during the first summer there only one team and wagon passed their camp: a family of Indians who looked at them curiously but did not make a sound. In her autobiographical account of these years, she calls the area a "frontier":

> I used the word "frontier" intentionally. I know now that the life we saw in those years was the end of the last frontier. The north end of the Lower Peninsula of Michigan was far from the early routes of migration to the West, across the Appalachians and down the Ohio Valley. The early fur traders in Canada had their own routes north of the Great Lakes. Mackinac had been a fort in the days of the fur trade, even before the Revolution, but the interior of the peninsula was almost unknown to white men before the logging industry began. [22]

In 1917 Ansley suffered a physical and mental breakdown, brought on in part by his struggle over the direction he wished the Department of English to take. [23] He resigned his position at the University, sold his Iowa City home, and moved his family to the Michigan land. His physical and mental state allowed him to do little work for over a year, but the rest was therapeutic, and he soon began writing Frederick and others optimistically about his life of pioneering. The following excerpt, from a 1917 letter to W. A. Jessup, president of the University of Iowa, suggests that Ansley was an enthusiastic proselytizer:

> Possibly friendship leads you now and then to consider for a moment about the fortunes of my wife, my children and myself in our pioneering. I shall tell you something of these fortunes as I see them.
>
> On the whole, farming has so far been kinder to us than we expected or could reasonably expect. We are in good health, all more vigorous than when we came. The larger things here are more right than we knew, although the region was not unknown to us. The climate is remarkably satisfactory. . . . The soil is proving good, so that most settlers have grown content. Regularly, they are trying to buy more land. Roads are noticeably improving. . . . We usually see several [settlers] in a day

pass our camp where a few years ago we might see a wagon once a fortnight. Markets are not bad. The wool from my sheep sold for sixty-four cents a pound. . . .

. . . After marl and alfalfa, so far everything, even corn, has yielded remarkably well. The farm, once isolated, is on the way to becoming accessible, as I expected when I bought it. [24]

Hearing this kind of report, both Frederick and his father were so taken with the idea of pioneering that in the spring of 1919 they pooled their resources and bought 1,400 acres of land adjoining Ansley's which included two small lakes, woodland, pasture, and 200 acres of farm land. (They paid a dollar an acre for some portions of the tract.) Soon they were clearing more woodland; raising cattle, sheep, and alfalfa; and building a large stone house with their own hands.

While Frederick was getting his farm established, the work of *Midland* had to be done, as he told his readers, in the brief intervals of "building and of clearing and plowing the land" (20.56). The "Contributors Note" in the issue for August-September, 1922 — summer issues were sometimes bimonthly [25] — makes it clear that the work of building the farm was lightened by the fellowship and sometimes even the hands of visiting writers and associate editors:

NELSON ANTRIM CRAWFORD has been an associate editor of *The Midland* from its foundation, and . . . is a frequent contributor to *The Dial, Poetry,* and other literary magazines. During the present summer he spent some days at Glennie and joined in the haymaking and other activities of the editor's farm.

RAYMOND KNISTER, of Blenheim, Ontario, contributed a story to the first number of *The Midland* for the present year. He too visited Glennie during the summer. (8.280)

Frederick lived year-round at Glennie for only two years, but the wilderness farm became what one *Midland* contributor, Warren Van Dine, has called the "permanent spiritual home" of the magazine. The Fredericks returned there each summer, often bringing with them people connected with *Midland*. Once, the Fredericks took a young *Midland* writer, Evelyn Harter, with them in June, kept her with them through the summer, and then found her a teaching job in the neighborhood for the winter. Edwin Ford Piper spent a couple of summers there, and most other associate editors and frequent contributers sooner or later made, as Mott called it, a "pilgrimage" there to "live and work a while in the visitors' cottage." [26] In the evenings, after the work of the farm was completed, there would be long discussions about manuscripts and other business of the magazine. During these times Glennie must have taken on much of the atmosphere of a literary colony, especially when Ansley was there and another neighbor, Walter Muilenburg, walked over to join the group.

Muilenburg, Frederick's exclassmate, whose early stories in *Midland* had attracted Edward J. O'Brien's attention, had bought a tract of land adjoining Frederick's, built a log cabin there, and become something of a recluse. He had started by living in his cabin only in the summers, but soon quit his teaching job and took up permanent residence in the woods, where he spent his time hunting, fishing, raising sheep, and writing. One evening in the summer of 1924, after returning from a gathering at Frederick's farm, he wrote his brother a long letter in which he talked about gathering wild raspberries and blackberries for jam and wine, listening to Dvorak and Schubert on his portable Victrola, and dynamiting stumps on his land "when in a celebrating mood." Since moving permanently to the woods, he wrote, the "writing itch" had come back to him:

> To most people this hermit life would be eerie; to me it is ideal. . . . I have all of the advantages that Thoreau brought out in his *Walden,* and a number he never enjoyed: to wit, good food and good tobacco. Thoreau put his idea in my head, and the matter has worked out with wonderful satisfaction. . . . I have been able to write between one and two thousand words easily in an evening.[27]

The kind of life Muilenburg led must have been tempting to many Glennie visitors tied to the routine of university jobs.

Soon after Frederick quit his teaching job at Moorhead, he began working on two novels which, according to a recent book, reflect "the first really significant expression of this positive approach to the farm."[28] The Glennie influence was reflected in *Midland* as well. While Frederick was living year-round at the wilderness farm and walked or drove "the three miles to the box where the rural mail carrier leaves manuscripts and receives the grain-bags filled with magazines" (7.111), he wrote leisurely editorial essays on such topics as his day-long wagon drives over log roads, the beauty and "exquisite symmetry" of the breaking plough, and the coming of autumn. When he returned to the farm only in the summers, the pastoral mode continued, even in the change of address notices:

> When this issue of *The Midland* reaches its readers, the editor will have returned to his home at Glennie. Contributions and other communications intended for the editor should be sent to him at Glennie, Alcona Co., Michigan. . . . Business letters should be sent to the

publication office at Iowa City, Iowa.

The wilderness has a friendly welcome for him who returns. Hills and fields and woodlands have the familiar sweetness of an old home. The colorful, brush-clad slopes are still hushed by winter. Their quiet is restful, strengthening, making for courage. Earth has healing for bodies and souls of those who love her. (8.112)

A rural orientation remained a part of the magazine. In one editorial Frederick questioned whether "the race can survive if the centripetal force of industry keeps crowding the population into cities." The nostalgic tone of that editorial suggests perhaps better than anything else the frustration the editors of *Midland* must have felt at the increasing urbanization of American society:

The older American writer, like Americans of an earlier generation, was typically a man or woman familiar with farm and village life, acquainted with occupations and emotions intimately related to the earth. His study window opened on the fields. Sky, soil, and sun were real to him.

But to the new generation of urban Americans, and to the writers among these especially, the apartment, the subway, the pavement are the realities. Fields, forests, streams, are remote, figurative, not felt or understood. To a person whose whole life has been definitely urban, in the modern sense, many of the prevailing ideas of earlier literature are incomprehensible and absurd, and its very language is obsolete. What can such expressions as 'to dig deep,' 'to go to the roots of things,' 'to plough a straight furrow,' mean to a man who has never handled a spade, or set out a tree, or seen a plough? (14.152)

Return to Iowa:1921-1930

BY 1921 Frederick was faced with the prospect of having to give up *Midland*. Since the magazine's first year when it ended $263.61 in the red, Frederick had had to make up annual deficits from his own pocket. When postwar deflation began to affect severely his farm income, he found that he did not really have enough to support his family, much less the magazine. His neighbor Ansley, now recovered in health but

unable to make enough from farming to support his family, had just left
his farm to edit a farm journal published in Lincoln, Nebraska. Because
that journal, *The New State,* had a leftist orientation, Ansley was soon
blacklisted by the universities and, thereafter, was unable to find a
teaching job. Eventually he did find a temporary position with the New
School of Social Research in New York, and by the end of the twenties
had worked himself up to editor-in-chief of the Columbia University
Press. While there he achieved probably his greatest distinction by
conceiving of and editing the one-volume *Columbia Encyclopaedia,*
advertised as the first encyclopaedia written from an American view-
point. But in 1921 Ansley was not in a position to be of much help to
Midland.

Frederick's first plan was to try to supplement what he could make at
his Glennie farm by arranging winter lecture tours to speak on contemporary American literature. Thinking he would be especially welcome at the University of Iowa, he wrote President Jessup:

> I am planning to make a trip in Iowa and adjoining states in the
> winter of 1921-22, lecturing on 'The Middle West in American Lit-
> erature.' I have already arranged to speak at . . . several places.
>   . . . Would there be a chance that I might come to the University
> regularly each winter as a lecturer on various phases of American
> literature, particularly the contemporary field, appearing several
> times each season? Thus I might become a member of the faculty
> again, though in a humble capacity and at modest remuneration, and
> The Midland might be again associated with the institution which
> fostered it.[29]

When the chairman of the Department of English was shown this letter,
he advised Jessup that he wanted Frederick to come as a regular faculty
member and argued that

> some organization agreeable to Mr. Frederick and giving him proper
> authority should be created which would definitely affiliate The
> Midland with this department and the University so that it would
> not remain a mere private enterprise on our campus.[30]

This was the sticking point. Frederick had suggested in his letter that
Midland might again be "associated" with the institution which fostered
it, but Frederick did not want any *formal* affiliation. After some bar-
gaining Frederick finally struck an agreement with President Jessup
satisfactory to himself. He would return to the university as a regular
faculty member but would remain free to have a semester off each year
to pursue the work of his farm, the magazine, and his own writing.

The university would provide office space and a part-time student assistant for *Midland*, but the relationship would end there: the magazine would retain its complete editorial independence and receive no financial support from the university. This arrangement lasted until 1930, except for one year when Frederick left Iowa to teach at the University of Pittsburgh.

Since regional magazines established later—such as *The Prairie Schooner* at the University of Nebraska and *The Frontier* at the University of Montana—were closely affiliated with universities, Frederick's desire to keep *Midland* independent may seem somewhat puzzling. The reason undoubtedly had much to do with the place of American literature in the universities at the time. Frederick has recalled that when he began *Midland* in 1915 at least one of the more respected members of the English department at Iowa, Professor E. N. S. Thompson, had been "amused" that anyone would devote his time not only to American literature but to contemporary American literature. At the time, literary study in America was still very much under the influence of German scholarship and heavily oriented toward philology. Relatively little study was given to works written later than the seventeenth century. In the standard, year-long English literature course Frederick had taken as an undergraduate the professor had covered up to "The Battle of Malden" by the end of the first semester; in the second semester he covered Chaucer, Shakespeare, Milton, and then skipped to one Dickens novel. During the 1920s, as Howard Mumford Jones has pointed out in *The Theory of American Literature,*

> the rift between academic conservatism and American writing was deepened by the outpourings of the humanists . . . who not only demanded that colleges concentrate upon European geniuses long dead, but also expressed a militant hostility to most American writing past and present.[31]

It is not surprising, then, that Frederick, while living at Glennie, had warned *Midland* readers against "academicism, which misnames historical research as literary achievement. We believe that there are very many writers and readers in America who will welcome leadership out of . . . the desert of the schools" (7.60-61).

The University of Iowa was nonetheless a much more congenial place for *Midland* to be located than most other universities would have been during the twenties. A 1926 study of the MLA American Literature Group found that most colleges offering any American literature courses at all felt that one course was sufficient for their needs. Princeton University offered no courses in American literature, but was considering reviving a "course in American ideals, beginning with Milton, Burke, Paine, and continuing through Franklin, Emerson, Thoreau, and Whittier." Another study completed in 1928 found that American colleges offered as many courses in Scandinavian literature as in American literature. Moreover, they offered twice as many courses in Italian literature as in American literature, four times as many in French literature, and five times as many in both Latin and Greek literature.[32] But at Iowa, it had been the chairman of the Department of English in 1915, Ansley, who had been instrumental in starting *Midland* and who had assisted it in many ways. His replacement, Hardin Craig, proved almost as helpful to the magazine. Although primarily a Shakespearian scholar, Craig taught an American literature course at Iowa, supported *Midland* financially, argued for Frederick's return at a substantially higher salary than when he defected to Pittsburgh, and allowed Frederick to teach what was probably the first college course ever in contemporary American literature.[33] Craig even supported Frederick in a rather serious controversy involving Sherwood Anderson.

On Frederick's return to the University of Iowa in 1921, he organized the "Saturday Luncheon Club," an unofficial group that met in the dining room of Youde's Inn, a large, privately-owned Iowa City rooming house located just off campus on the north side of Calvin Hall. Each semester students paid five dollars for five lunches and five lectures by contemporary authors, including many *Midland* writers as well as more famous ones, such as Robert Frost and Carl Sandburg. From the beginning the club was immensely successful. In 1925, when it had more than three hundred members, Frederick invited Sherwood Anderson, who had published *Many Marriages* two years before and *Dark Laughter* that same year—both somewhat controversial books at the time. As was customary, Frederick asked the local bookstores to stock copies of these books well in advance of the lecture so that club members could read and discuss them. Certain townspeople saw the books in the bookstores, learned that Anderson was coming to lecture, and demanded that Frederick cancel the lecture to prevent Sherwood Anderson from planting seeds of sexual revolution in Iowa City. Some pressure was exerted on President Jessup to fire Frederick if he should persist in his plans. But Hardin Craig strongly backed Frederick's decision to go ahead with the lecture. Anderson came and gave what one listener, Alma Hovey, describes as a "very mild" talk. After that, Frederick's Saturday Luncheon Club prospered as never before, so much so that it was soon regularly outdrawing the officially sponsored university lecture series.

Frederick remained at the University of Iowa for the rest of the twenties. But during all that time *Midland* remained a "mere private enterprise" on the campus. And the fact that the magazine's editorial office was located in the basement of old University Hall (now Jessup Hall) did not prevent the editors from continuing to give a somewhat anti-academic cast to the magazine, as the following comment in 1927 indicates:

> . . . these sixty pages told me more about what the [short] story has been, is, and is likely to be, than I had found in a score of fat, analytical volumes by thin, synthetic professors. (13.127)

H. L. Mencken and Frank Luther Mott

Two men, each in a different way, were of even more importance to *Midland* during the twenties than was Hardin Craig. One, H. L. Mencken, the sage of Baltimore, did for the magazine in the twenties what Edward J. O'Brien had done for it in the teens.

As different as Mencken's background and temperament were from Frederick's, some of their ideas were remarkably similar. In 1920, for instance, Mencken wrote in *The Nation* about the pernicious influence New York exerted on the young writer who went there:

> His ideas are delicately flattened out. He learns to do things as they should be done. New York swarms with such wrecks of talents—men who arrived with one or two promising books behind them, and are now highly respectable inmates of publishers' bordellos.

Mencken went on to call the city that printed "four-fifths of the books of the nation and nine-tenths of its magazines" hardly American at all, "huge, Philistine, self-centered, ignorant and vulgar." The real literary center of America, he wrote, was the Middle West:

> With two exceptions, there is not a single American novelist of the younger generation—that is, a serious novelist, a novelist deserving a civilized reader's notice—who has not sprung from the Middle Empire that has Chicago for its capital.[34]

So it is not surprising that when Frederick sent Mencken some stories for consideration in *The Smart Set* shortly after the above quotation appeared, Mencken greeted him warmly and began a relationship whose importance for *Midland* would be hard to overestimate.

Walter Lippmann later called Mencken the most powerful influence on a whole generation of educated people; by 1920 he was already a formidable critic who had helped establish the reputations of Theodore Dreiser, Willa Cather, and Sherwood Anderson. The first thing he did to help *Midland*'s reputation was to write Frederick that "the *Midland* is full of excellent stuff" and then to tell him he could use the comment for promotional purposes. Frederick did. Mencken also took an interest in Frederick's own writing, carefully criticized his work, printed four of his stories in *Smart Set,* and suggested he send his first novel to Alfred Knopf, the innovative young publisher who was to publish Mencken's *American Mercury* beginning in 1924. When Knopf received Frederick's novel, he showed it to Mencken. Mencken liked it and Knopf published it. In the next few years Knopf also published *Stories from the Midland,* edited by Frederick, Frederick's *A Handbook of Short Story Writing,* and another Frederick novel—the proceeds from all directly or indirectly supporting *Midland.*

When Mencken reviewed Frederick's first novel, *Druida,* in *Smart Set,* his remarks about the book were generally positive. But his review, which ended as follows, surely promoted Frederick's magazine more than it ever did his novel:

> The author is a college professor of English, but amazingly unlike his colleagues of that faculty. At a time when most of the rest of them, particularly in the Middle West, were diligently editing texts of Bayard Taylor and John Greenleaf Whittier for the use of sophomores, and violently endeavoring to graft the decaying New England tradition upon the Western stem, he founded a free magazine for the encouragement of the younger native authors of the region, and set out to hunt for talent in the tall grass. . . . Altogether, his little magazine, the *Midland* . . . is probably the most influential literary periodical ever set up in America though its actual circulation has always been small. (*The Smart Set,* July 1923, p. 141)

Mencken favored the magazine with this hyperbole partly because he thought so highly of *Midland* writers Frederick had already steered in his direction. In 1918 Frederick had printed the first published work of the Iowa writer Ruth Suckow—a slight but delicate quatrain. Later he printed several of her stories and arranged for her to come to Iowa City to have more time to write and to assist him with the magazine. He advised her to send some of her work to Mencken, to whom he wrote that he believed "profoundly in her capacity, as I do in her achievement."[35]When Mencken saw her stories he liked them, began publishing her in *Smart Set,* featured her in the opening issue of his *American Mercury* (along with Leonard Cline, another *Midland* contributor), and continued to champion her work throughout the twenties.

We can never be certain about matters of influence, but we may be sure that Mencken's 1923 boost in *Smart Set* and subsequent good words for *Midland* in and out of print did nothing to harm its reputation. By 1925, in a promotional folder, Frederick was able to list plaudits for his magazine from eighteen other sources, including *The Double Dealer, The Literary Digest, The Literary Review, Poetry,* and *The Saturday Review of Literature.*

Edward J. O'Brien, also, continued to look kindly on *Midland.* In the late teens he had begun to rate magazines according to the quality of their fiction. During the twenties *Midland* usually came at or very near the top of his list. In 1926, for instance, O'Brien's list went as follows:

"Rank by percentage of distinctive stories"

1	Dial	100%
2	Midland	100%
3	Forum	100%
4	Harper's Magazine	97%
5	Atlantic Monthly	95%
6	American Mercury	94%
7	Century Magazine	93%
8	Vanity Fair	92%
9	Scribner's Magazine	73%
10	Pictorial Review	68%
	. . . .	
17	Red Book Magazine	34%
18	Good Housekeeping	34%
19	Collier's Weekly	29%
20	Ladies' Home Journal	25%
21	McCalls Magazine	24%
22	Liberty	23%
23	Saturday Evening Post	22%

O'Brien also denoted with three stars the stories he considered worth reprinting in book form, and he included some of these in his annual collection. Throughout the twenties he three-starred many *Midland* stories, sometimes reprinting as many as three in a single volume. Because of this, some writers who could probably have gotten money for their stories from other magazines sent them to Frederick in hopes of getting an O'Brien accolade.

By 1925 Frederick was receiving ten or a dozen manuscripts each day and finding that he simply could no longer keep up with the work. To alleviate things he asked Frank Luther Mott to serve with him as coeditor. Mott proved a good choice.

Mott had enthusiastically followed *Midland* from its first issue when he was editor of a small-town weekly newspaper in Grand Junction, Iowa. In 1917 he had written a series of articles for his newspaper entitled "Six Prophets Out of the Midwest"; the first five articles were on individual authors such as Hamlin Garland, but the last was on *Midland.* Although that article came to Frederick's attention in 1917, he did not really get to know Mott until 1920 when Mott sent him a story to consider for *Midland.* Mott later recalled the incident in an article:

> I sent it ["The Man with the Good Face"] to a New York literary agent named Holly, with a two-dollar reading fee; and he replied as follows: 'I regret to report that I cannot see a sale for it. . . . It has an unhealthy and morbid theme.' But John Frederick did not agree. He immediately accepted the story for the *Midland,* made a few helpful suggestions for improvements . . . , and published it in his magazine in December, 1920. Then Edward J. O'Brien reprinted it in his *Best Short Stories* volume for 1921, and anthologists picked it up from there, and so on. [36]

When an opening later developed on the Iowa faculty, Frederick helped persuade Hardin Craig to hire Mott, who already had a B.A. from the University of Chicago and an M.A. from Columbia University where he had written a thesis on Iowa dialects. Soon after his arrival in Iowa City, Mott began helping Frederick with both the Saturday Luncheon Club and *Midland.* When Mott became coeditor in 1925 he brought to the magazine a new energy, a new aggressiveness, and a personality that in many ways complemented Frederick, who—Mott once wrote— "maintained always a certain modest reserve of dignity." [37]

By nature Mott was outgoing. When he was a young man he had seen some poems by Vachel Lindsay in *The Independent* and "struck up a correspondence with him." [38] And after first reading John G. Neihardt, he "got on a train and went to Bancroft, Nebraska, to see and talk with him." Mott spent several summers lecturing about American literature on the Chautauqua circuit, and the experience served him well when he began speaking to groups in Iowa and surrounding states about contemporary literature and *Midland.*

The coeditors alternated writing the section of brief book reviews, now called "I've Been Reading." Mott always lent variety to the department, often reflecting in his choice of books his enthusiasm for black literature—which he had developed when he was at Columbia and had glimpsed signs of the renaissance in Harlem—and for the history of American magazines—the subject of his doctoral dissertation and his later, definitive, five-volume work.

Mott wrote that there was never a happier partnership. "The editors agreed basically in theory and nearly always in taste and differed enough to make them check on one another."[39] They shared the task of first reader, passed on to the other any manuscripts which they thought had possibilities, and met weekly to make decisions. It was a very pleasant arrangement for Frederick, too, who suddenly found himself freed from half the work.

Midland and the Young Writer

THE importance of *Midland* for many writers from the Midwest and other regions is hard to overestimate. Paul Engle, longtime head of the Iowa Writers Workshop (now director of the International Writing Program), recalls that when he first saw a copy of *Midland* as a school-boy in Cedar Rapids, Iowa, he was struck by the fact that it was unlike any of the magazines he had ever seen, unlike the ones that his mother read, or that he could buy in local drugstores. He had discovered not only a midwestern medium that took contemporary fiction seriously, but also a place where he could send his own work and have it sensitively criticized. Throughout most of *Midland*'s history every single manuscript received was returned with a handwritten note or an individually typed letter by Frederick or one of his assistants.[40] This task was monumentally time-consuming, but as one editor wrote in his little magazine in 1927,

> Frederick is patient as Griselda, hopeful as Penthesilea. The cataract of manuscript never wearies him. He is tolerant of letter writers and advice seekers. He will read the most unattractive looking stuff, I am told, thinking himself well repaid if he finds one grain of good in a ton of chaff.[41]

More than anything else, it was this incredible patience and hopefulness that made Frederick such a necessary editor for *Midland*, and *Midland* such a valuable magazine for young writers.

A writer who showed any talent at all got encouragement and the request to see more of his work. If a story or a poem seemed as if it might be improved enough through revision to be seriously considered for publication, it would receive detailed criticism. The length and nature of this criticism varied, of course, but the following two excerpts from letters [42] indicate the care with which criticism was often given and the seriousness with which it, no doubt, was usually received:

Dear Beadle:

. . . The most important thing to revise is the burlesque accident in connection with the trousers at the middle of page six. I do not feel that this is quite giving the effect you want at this point in the story and I wonder if it is really a desirable thing to have here at all. Would it perhaps be better just to manage in some other way the necessary transition from one point of view to another in connection with passing through the door?

It is a mistake to move into an external point of view as you describe the old man on page four and also in the eighth line on page seven. I think the reader will be better satisfied making his own picture of the old man particularly since you introduce your description so late.

There are several sentences which need smoothing but it is needless to say that this story has to be just right or it will not succeed at all. I believe you can make it so, however, and am much interested in the story. I hope that you will let me see it again.

(Letter from Frederick to John Beadle)

Dear Mr. Mott:

Here is 'The Joker,' erstwhile 'Triumph,' which I have reworked along the lines of your suggestion. You were perfectly right to see that the plot (melodramatic for an unworthy purpose) was of much less importance than the theme and the chief character. As I have reworked the story, I think the theme comes out more clearly than before. . . .

(Letter from Philip Stevenson to Mott)

The stories referred to in these letters went through several revisions. Neither was ever published in *Midland* because Frederick, who usually felt that he had more good material than space in which to print it, could afford to be exacting. And exacting *Midland* was, even with writers the editors knew personally and published regularly, such as Marie Gilchrist, a Cleveland poet:

Dear Miss Gilchrist:

I am returning 'Lost Sounds' at the request of the editors who want the poem but object to the Briticism, 'spate.' With this word changed the poem will be entirely available for The Midland. I enclose herewith, too, the unavailable poems.[43]

At least one author who achieved some later success, MacKinlay Kantor, feels that Frederick was perhaps too exacting or, at least, made some wrong editorial choices:

True, he did publish a few of my verses in *The Midland;* but I wasn't able to suit him with a single line of prose. . . . A glance at the records shows me that he turned down *Lyman Dillon And His Plough, Big Jonas,* and other offerings which found repute years afterward. There was even one little number entitled *Daydream In A Buckskin Age,* which I incorporated in one of those pioneer incidents appearing in SPIRIT LAKE, decades after it was sent back to me by Mr. Frederick.[44]

The important thing was that Frederick kept young writers with promise working, kept them striving to improve their work. Even his shortest notes—he invariably signed notes "Cordially yours"—reflect his sure understanding that a beginning author needs praise, blunt criticism, and encouragement, always in that order:

Dear Mr. Derleth:

This has genuine reality and accomplishes a great deal in its 3,000 words. I believe, however, that it needs a slightly richer treatment—somewhat fuller detail. The first part of it I found a little dull.

I hope to see something else of yours soon.

Cordially yours,

(Signed) John T. Frederick [45]

No one knows how many writers received encouragement from *Midland,* but more than likely those who actually published in the magazine represent only the tip of the iceberg. There are no records extant of manuscripts received before 1931. But the incomplete records that exist from 1931-33 suggest that there are many writers today who were never actually published in *Midland* but who sent Frederick their manuscripts when they were young enough to profit from his careful editorial advice.[46] Five years after *Midland* ceased publication, one such writer, Wallace Stegner, wrote the following in *The Saturday Review of Literature:*

In effect, John T. Frederick and his friends on *The Midland* did for fiction, through the little magazine, what Susan Glaspell and George Cram Cook [leaders of the Provincetown Players] had done for drama through the little theatre. But the regional flavor . . . of Frederick's magazine . . . and the fact that his work had been done in and for Iowa and the Middle West, have made this unselfish and helpful critic and editor the greatest single force in Iowa letters in the past twenty-five years. [47]

Time colors the memory. But recent statements [48] by writers who did publish in *Midland* at least serve to corroborate what Stegner wrote about Frederick in 1938. John G. Neihardt, whom Frederick published in 1915, wrote that a new writer felt a great deal of prestige when he appeared in *Midland*'s pages because of the journal's "exceptional" editor. August Derleth, who went on to publish more than one hundred novels after Frederick first published him in 1933 (after an initial exchange of *eighty* letters with the young writer about his work!), said that *Midland* did "yeoman service in encouraging the writing of some of our best regional material." Comments from writers who were published in *Midland* in other years are of the same nature:

> John T. Frederick whom I never met was a great encourager of writing, not only regional writing. . . . I remember the magazine and the editor with the kind of glow that only a good man can radiate across time.
>
> Benjamin Appel

> Frederick was . . . so understanding, so sympathetic and encouraging of efforts that must have often seemed amateurish and naive. . . . There was a time when I thought that I would stay at the University of Iowa and try to be a more serious writer rather than a journalist, and the reason was largely Frederick and the inspiration that he offered.
>
> Marquis Childs

> I doubt if I could emphasize too strongly the influence John T. Frederick has had on my writing . . . THE MIDLAND opened doors for me that I never suspected would open.
>
> James Hearst

Midland also served the interests of young writers in less direct ways. By its very success it encouraged men in other regions of the country to attempt something similar. In *Understanding Magazines,* Raymond Wolseley states that *Midland* "inspired *The Prairie Schooner* and *The*

Frontier,[49] regional magazines founded at the Universities of Nebraska and Montana. While there is no evidence that *Midland* "inspired" the remarkable group of Southern poets to begin a journal for their work, Frederick's magazine probably did serve indirectly to encourage their efforts. For in 1922 Witter Bynner, a poet who had already published in *Midland* twice and who would continue corresponding with the editors, happened to hear a group of men read their poetry in a friend's home in Nashville, Tennessee. Bynner suggested that if they would begin publishing a journal for their work, they would quickly find an audience; they took his advice and started *The Fugitive.*[50]

Whenever new magazines were established in other regions, the audience of a *Midland* writer increased, since Frederick exchanged magazine copies with any new magazine he heard about. The exchange system, in fact, was apparently widespread among all little magazines of the time, and especially among the regionally oriented ones. Henry Nash Smith, associate editor of *The Southwest Review* from 1927 until 1942, said that the editors of that magazine "read all the regional journals we could lay hands on as a matter of policy and felt ourselves to be part of an unorganized regional movement."[51] Because *Midland* was the first, and one of the strongest regional little magazines of that era, it served as a model for other journals and played at least some part in keeping that "movement" going.

An "Uncommercial Magazine With an Impecunious Publisher"

IN an article on "Small Magazines" published in 1930, Ezra Pound wrote that "the significance of any work of art or literature is a root significance that goes down into its original motivation. When this motivation is merely a desire for money . . . there occurs a pervasive monotony in the product corresponding to the underlying monotony in the motivation."[52] For the editors of *Midland,* as for Pound, this idea was so fundamental that they reiterated it with regularity. The subject first came up in the first sentence of *Midland's* first editorial:

The Midland is not a commercial enterprise, and it is not endowed. Its publishers, editors and contributors receive no payment for their work. Obviously, miscellaneous advertising is not sought or accepted. Possibly subscriptions will meet the only expenses of the magazine — the cost of printing and mailing. With that faint hope its commercialism ends. (1.1)

In an editorial written "After Five Years" Frederick stated that although financial returns had been possible more than once if *Midland* had wanted to become "an organ" for advertisers, that option had always been turned down because the magazine's "endeavor toward service would inevitably have been compromised" (6.2). The only treasure *Midland* had sought, he said, was one that "includes freedom, a blessed thing, granted by good Saint Francis and his gracious Lady Poverty." The cadence continued the next year:

> There has been art known as Christian, art known as Franciscan; we have not yet seen the Fordian art, the Rockefellerian art. . . . Milton made his epics without assistance from the great ones of the time of Charles the Second other than that they forgot him. The Pilgrim's Progress was not helped by patronage. Samuel Johnson did some literary work without a patron; at least, he said he did. Some cathedrals were built under another inspiration. (7.294-295)

And the next:

> *The Midland* is not commercial. Its editor believes that a literary magazine, like a church or a school, should be governed by other considerations than those of profit. (7.37)

And in 1930:

> Somehow the febrile rhythm of competitive trade, that increasingly dominates our American literary life, must be checked or broken: for the sake of the many writers as yet unconquered by it, and the thousands of readers who deplore and resent it. To such writers and such readers I appeal for support of *The Midland,* to be given not in charity, but in comradeship. (16.60)

Unfortunately, unlike other non-commercial little magazines such as *Poetry* and *The Seven Arts, Midland* was never able to attract any significant financial backing. *Midland* remained, as Frederick put it, "an uncommercial magazine with an impecunious publisher" (7.327). He had hoped that the money from subscriptions would cover the cost of printing and mailing, but it never did. Each fall Frederick would have to decide whether he could afford to continue publishing for another year. Beginning in 1915 and continuing each year thereafter, he would advise his subscribers of the situation and would then appeal for their help:

Dear Friend:
    We are at present considering the advisability of continuing THE MIDLAND. The first year has resulted rather disastrously from a financial standpoint, and a heavy deficit has arisen.

At the end of 1918, when Frederick had accumulated a personal deficit of more than $500, he tried one of many ideas—ideas that were to occupy much of his time and energy—to get more money for the magazine. In a pamphlet entitled "Shall the Middle West Make its Rightful Contribution to American Literature?" he announced to subscribers and friends that

the editors have decided to undertake the establishment of a relatively stable fund for the extension and development of the magazine. The method adopted is that of sustaining subscriptions. Sustaining subscribers will pay twenty-five dollars annually for a period of three years, starting with 1919. . . .
    General adoption of the simple means of support thus provided will result in the enlargement of the magazine, and will make possible a steady constructive campaign for subscribers. The editors believe that if forty or more sustaining subscriptions can be procured, the magazine will make such progress within the period of three years as to have become entirely self-supporting.

Frederick probably never expected forty sustaining subscribers to be forthcoming (which would have given him $1,000 for three years) but he did expect more than the twelve recorded for 1919.[53]
    Two years earlier, he had begun another venture which he no doubt hoped eventually would become profitable for the magazine: The Midland Press. The first book published under the Press imprint was a book of poems, *Barbed Wire and Wayfarers,* which had originally appeared in the January, February, March, and April issues of the journal in 1917. This book went through three editions and its author, Edwin Ford Piper, donated a portion of his royalties to the magazine. But there is no evidence that writers whom the Midland Press published in subsequent years donated any of their royalty money to the magazine, or even realized any royalties. As a service for *Midland* writers, the Midland Press was a success; as a means of aiding the magazine financially, it failed.

The most remunerative idea Frederick ever had was to go on lecture tours. In 1925, for instance, he spoke during one trip at Pittsburgh, Baltimore, Washington, D. C., Dartmouth College, Michigan State, and Indiana University. Having received $50 or more for each appearance, he was able to pay off nearly half the $1,000 debt the magazine had at the time. A letter Frederick wrote a few years later to a professor at the University of Montana suggests that these tours were profitable in other ways, since they gave Frederick a chance to meet many young writers around the country. The letter also suggests that the financial arrangements for the lectures were fully in keeping with the noncommercial spirit of *Midland:*

May 4, 1928

Dear Professor Merriam: —

I have just returned from a lecturing trip in the East and find your good letters waiting for me. I am extremely happy to know that you feel that you can arrange for me to visit Missoula, and I shall look forward to that part of my trip with much more pleasure than to any other. Let me say in the first place that I do not want you to be embarrassed about the financial side of the arrangement, and if the amount which I suggested in my earlier letters proves burdensome, we will make it less. I am especially grateful for your efforts to help me to get engagements at other places in Montana. Of course if I can get these it will be especially easy to reduce my charge to the University if that will help. . . .

I spent the first three days of this week at Notre Dame where I shared the apartment of Professor C. A. Phillips. . . . I gave one general lecture open to all members of the student body, addressed two class groups in which several classes had been combined, had a long session with the Scribbler's Club, and met twenty or more boys in personal conference in connection with their writing. Something of this sort is what I shall hope to do when I come to you.

With kindest regards, I am

Cordially yours,

(Signed) John T. Frederick [54]

While Mott was coeditor from 1925-1930, he agreed to share with Frederick any debts *Midland* accumulated. But largely because of these trips the magazine was able to stay about even financially during these five years. Moreover, critical acclaim continued, the issues were a little thicker, and circulation edged upward. *Midland* was at last healthy in every way.

Midland in Chicago: 1930-1933

IN the first issue of 1930, Frederick announced that *Midland*'s subtitle would be changed from "A Magazine of the Middle West" to "A National Literary Magazine." This, he said, was in "somewhat belated recognition of the fact that almost from the beginning the material printed in the magazine has come from all parts of the country" (16.60). Up until that time—and this held roughly true for the magazine's remaining years—almost two-thirds of the contributors had come from midwestern states; but there were almost as many contributors from New York as from Illinois; more from California than from Michigan.

This change of subtitle came just before Edward J. O'Brien, in his 1930 preface to *Best Short Stories,* proposed a plan to make *Midland* a more potent force in national letters. O'Brien observed that the "quality" magazines were dying out — *The Century,* for example, had just ceased publication — because they had continued to offer stories recommended only by the canonized names of their authors.

> The true remedy for this lagging behind of the better monthlies is probably the establishment of a new national monthly in the Middle West which is nearer the present center of population. If I may venture a suggestion, I think the time is now ripe for *The Midland* to pool its interests with *The Prairie Schooner, The Frontier,* and perhaps one or two other regional periodicals such as *The Southwest Review,* and to issue a full-grown national monthly of belles-lettres in which short stories, poems, and essays should be given pride of place. The significance of such a new national periodical would depend very largely upon its interest in discovering new writers rather than in depending upon old ones.

O'Brien went on to suggest something that sounds somewhat strange to us today: that Iowa City, with *Midland,* might well surpass New York as the literary center of the United States:

> If *The Midland* chooses to take the lead in this matter, I am convinced, after many years' reflection, that it has the same opportunity to crystallize the best expression of contemporary national life that *The Atlantic Monthly* was able to seize upon its foundation, and that *Harper's Magazine* enjoyed a generation ago. Two generations ago Boston was the geographical centre of American literary

life, one generation ago New York could claim pride of place, and I trust that the idea will not seem too unfamiliar if I suggest that the geographical centre today is Iowa City.[55]

Frederick was very receptive to making a change with *Midland*, but not the kind of change O'Brien suggested. For one thing, Frederick was ready to break his ties with the University of Iowa and leave Iowa City; he found that teaching was taking up too much of his time, and he was disappointed with the direction the Department of English was taking. The year before, Hardin Craig had resigned as chairman of the department to go to Stanford University. On the day the announcement was made, Frederick had written the president of the university carefully spelling out his own position:

> The selection of Mr. Craig's successor will, it seems to me, involve a rather definite choice, as to the future policy of our English department, between increased service to the literary development of the state and of the region, on the one hand, and increased contribution to the general cause of academic research on the other.
>
> . . . .
>
> In recent years . . . the tendency in our English department has been toward increased emphasis upon philological investigation. It dominates our graduate work to the almost complete exclusion of creative effort. The natural effect is to fill the ranks of our instructors with men and women whose primary interests are in research, and this interest is of course expressed in their teaching. Within a few years, by the continuation of this process, our leadership in creative effort in our region will be lost.[56]

A memorandum in the Jessup papers shows that Frederick had recommended Edwin Ford Piper to replace Craig, and that Mott had recommended Frederick. The academic background of the man finally chosen, Baldwin Maxwell, no doubt indicated to Frederick in which direction the university had decided to move: out of twenty-seven graduate English courses Maxwell had taken, only one had been in literature past 1642.

Therefore, Frederick was not especially interested in remaining in Iowa City. Neither was he interested in O'Brien's suggestion of a merger. Actually, that suggestion was somewhat presumptuous on O'Brien's part since the other magazines he named were all relatively well-established and not inclined to give up their identity to become part of *Midland*.

In the summer of 1930, Frederick terminated his relationship with the University of Iowa and, he wrote, "with a box of subscription-cards and a sheaf of manuscripts — alike slender, sole impedimenta of the editorial office" — moved *Midland* to Chicago. In announcing the move to his readers, he assured them that it indicated no fundamental change in policy but was simply the latest tactic in *Midland's* overall strategy to challenge the ascendancy of New York:

> Chicago seems among American cities most likely to make a challenge to New York's domination immediately effective. Already the decentralization of the manufacture of books and magazines is far advanced, and the recent growth of the printing industry in the Chicago area has been very rapid. Further, Chicago has a literary tradition of high worth. It has *Poetry,* with its unparalleled achievement of eighteen years, and its continuing energy and vision. Chicago has produced many of the most important writers of our time — so many that a decade ago Mencken called it the new literary capital of America. . . .
>
> More important is the fact that Chicago is the logical permanent axis for a literary and cultural development of the United States as a whole, in which every region of the country shall have its rightful part. By lines of economic and cultural relationship, of which her radiating railroads are part and symbol, Chicago is so intimately connected with East and West and North and South alike that she could never become so stubbornly provincial as Boston was, so crassly provincial as New York now is. When American literature becomes truly American, representative of the life and expressive of the ideas and emotions of men and women in all parts of the country, its energies and achievements will focus in Chicago.
>
> . . . *The Midland* has been edited on real frontiers in Minnesota and Michigan, at the gateway between east and middle west at Pittsburgh, and in the relative quiet of a small university city in Iowa. Perhaps it needs Chicago in order to round out its reflection of the American scene. (16.370-71)

At first *Midland* in Chicago looked as if it might indeed become the kind of national force O'Brien had prophesied it could. Frederick had the advice of advertising men free of charge and circulation quickly went over a thousand. In a 1931 letter to subscribers he spoke of reaching "5,000 or 10,000 readers in America who would value *Midland.*" He began receiving a much larger offering of manuscripts and adopted a quarto-sized page to accommodate some of the new material. And in the *Best Short Stories* volume covering most of 1931, *Midland* was rated first in the number of distinctive short stories published (43), well above *Harper's, The North American Review,* and Mencken's *American Mercury.*

Just being located in Chicago was an asset for the magazine, because most serious midwestern writers sooner or later drifted there. Many of them dropped by *Midland*'s tiny quarters on the eighth floor of the Monadnock Building on West Jackson Street, making the office an exciting, busy place. Every morning for about six weeks, James T. Farrell, described in a *Midland* note as "a young Chicago writer," came by the office just to talk to whoever was around. Since Farrell had no money, Esther Frederick, who was assuming more and more of the duties of the magazine, usually ended up taking him to lunch.

Yet Frederick, always a very modest person, never really became part of the Chicago literary scene. He was more at home on his Glennie farm or in the Iowa City *Midland* office that looked out on huge elms down the slope to the Iowa River. Paul Engle recalls how harried and different Frederick looked when he first saw him in the Chicago office, which gave out on concrete and asphalt. And before Frederick had a chance to acclimate himself to the change, the Depression began moving westward. This was much to the surprise of Frederick and most other midwesterners who had assumed the Depression was a temporary phenomenon affecting the eastern seaboard. Since the little magazines subsisted on the economic fringe, they were quick to feel its effects. As early as 1930, in fact, an article had predicted an end to the entire little magazine movement:

> Last spring, in exile, *The Little Review* brought out its final number; the *Dial* survived for a few months only; and others, with limp stride and shortened breath, hover on the brink of the grave. . . . It would seem as if another chapter in our literary history—one of the liveliest and most colorful—is rounding to a close. [57]

By the end of 1931 Chicago was feeling the full effects of the Depression. As *The Little Magazine* states, "banks failed, bread lines grew, factories closed, business collapsed. *The Midland* was doomed." [58] The money from lectures and guarantors Frederick had relied on to keep the magazine solvent in the late twenties was no longer available.

Frederick had earlier told his readers: "I have not learned that, in a good cause, the certainty of defeat is a sufficient reason for refusing the fight" (8.296). In late 1931 he fought every way he knew to keep *Midland* going. He reduced office expenses by sharing quarters with another firm. Esther Frederick, now coeditor, spent more of her time with the magazine, reducing the expense of clerical assistance and allowing Frederick more time to work on promotional efforts around Chicago. And Frederick held part-time teaching jobs at Northwestern

University and Notre Dame, where he commuted twice a week. His determination was no doubt increased by the knowledge that there were fewer and fewer noncommercial magazines left; Loren Eiseley has recalled that during that period it was *Midland* and a few other regional journals that "helped to keep young writers active and interested . . . when it was almost impossible to get attention elsewhere."[59]

Finally Frederick turned, of course, to his readers. In a "frank statement of a crisis in the affairs of *The Midland*," he spelled out the dismal situation in a letter on 10 September 1931. That year alone the magazine would cost him more than $2,000, he said, and he did not feel he could risk adding to the deficit already accumulated. The letter is interesting both for its unfounded optimism and its understanding, personal tone:

> I believe that *The Midland* is truly unique among American literary magazines in having survived for seventeen years without endowment and without dependence on advertising.
>
> . . . Altogether, it seems possible that if we could weather the depression, greater use and value for the magazine in every way might lie beyond. . . .
>
> In making these suggestions [that subscribers renew their subscriptions and donate money if they were able] I want to say that I fully understand that many of those who are most interested in the magazine are very definitely unable to contribute to its support, especially at the present time. I know that some cannot promise even the renewal of their subscriptions. I want such readers to know that I recognize and appreciate their loyalty to the magazine none the less because they cannot express it in money. I hope that all readers will understand the necessity which has led to this appeal, and the spirit in which I make it.

This letter and the publicity *Midland* received because of it—Frederick's picture appeared, incongruously, in *Time* over the caption "Rating: high. Funds: low."—attracted just enough subscribers for Frederick to decide to keep publishing, at least for another year.[60]

By the end of 1932 subscriptions had plummeted to four hundred. Frederick published an issue dated January-February 1933, with the hope that money would turn up from some unexpected source. But none did; he held off publishing a second issue. In May when his debt was over $3,000 and no money was even in sight, he decided that the next issue would have to be his last. He telegraphed Lowry Wimberly at the University of Nebraska, editor of *The Prairie Schooner*, asking if he could "absorb" *Midland* by taking over its unexpired subscription list.[61] Wimberly had to turn down Frederick's offer because he was not sure his magazine would receive the university appropriation necessary to continue. Frederick then made a similar offer to H. G. Merriam at the University of Montana, editor of *The Frontier*, who accepted.

Midland's last issue was mailed out in early June of 1933 and dated March-April, May-June. Perhaps the most fitting eulogy for the magazine had been written by Frederick himself, in the opening editorial more than eighteen years before:

> Dying, the Venerable Bede repeated the words of Saint Ambrose: 'I have not lived so as to be ashamed to live among you; nor do I fear to die.' When *The Midland* dies, late or soon, may it die unashamed and leave pleasant memories. (1.2)

NOTES

1 *The Little Magazine* (Princeton, 1946), p. 3.
2 See *Midland,* Vol. 6, p. 3 (hereafter cited as 6.3).
3 Biographical information for Frederick can be found in *Who's Who*, 1926-27 (Chicago, 1926), p. 747; and *Current Biography*, 1941 (New York, 1941), pp. 309-11. Information here is based partly on interviews with Frederick and others.
4 Interview with Bruce Mahan, 17 February 1972.
5 This excerpt from Royce's speech is taken from *The Little Magazine,* p. 133.
6 Biographical information for Ansley may be found in *Who's Who,* 1938-39, and in a captivating autobiographical account by Ansley's daughter, Delight Ansley: *First Chronicles* (Doylestown, Pa., 1971). Information here is based partly on interviews with Alice Delight Ansley, John T. Frederick, and others.
7 *Athelney,* issued by Athelney Club, 1914, in the collection of the Iowa State Historical Society, Iowa City.
8 Pamphlet entitled *The Midland,* in Iowa collection. The most thorough study of the earlier magazine is by Louella M. Wright, "The Midland Monthly," *Iowa Journal of History and Politics* 45 (January 1947): 3-61.
9 *Iowa City Daily Press,* 6 January 1915, p. 2.
10 *Midland* 18.36. In the middle of 1931 the magazine went to a quarto page "in response to the demands of utility." In the first issue after the change Frederick wrote briefly about the typographical history of *Midland* and gave special praise to Springer. Springer's large book collection is now a part of the University of Iowa Libraries.
11 "News Notes," *Poetry* 42 (July 1933): 238.
12 In *A History of American Magazines: 1905-1930* (Cambridge, Mass., 1968), p. 179, Frank Luther Mott lists the following ten people as *Midland* associate editors for a period of more than five years: Ansley, 1915-29; Sergel, 1915-28; McPeak, 1915-23 (editor, May-June 1916); Piper, 1915-1930; Esther Frederick, 1915-1930 (coeditor, 1930-33); Crawford, 1917-29; Alexander, 1918-28; Chawner, 1918-28; Tower, 1921-28 and Mott, 1921-25 (coeditor 1925-30). Seven others served as associate editors for shorter periods of time: Raymond H. Durboraw, 1915-18; Percival Hunt, 1918-20; Weare Holbrook, 1918-22; Ruth Suckow, 1921-22; George Carver, 1923-28; and Raymond Knister, 1923-24.
13 Frederick later wrote a short article on Piper entitled, "A Maker of Songs," *American Prefaces* 2 (March 1937):83-84; that issue was devoted solely to Piper's work.
14 The "guarantors" are listed in a prepublication pamphlet, *Statement of Purpose and Organization of The Midland,* which is included in the Iowa collection. The other

guarantors listed are C. F. Ansley, Raymond H. Durboraw, Ival McPeak, Roger L. Sergel, John T. Frederick, E. S. Thompson, Esther Paulus, Hoyt Cooper, and Thomas H. Macbride.

15   The farm, now run by a fifth-generation Paulus, may be the oldest family farm in Iowa. It was originally purchased by Conrad Paulus from the U.S. Government in 1860. John Frederick now lives there with his second wife; after Esther died he married her sister-in-law who lived on the farm and whose own husband had just died.

16   Letter from Ruth Suckow to Frederick, 16 October 1931; Ruth Suckow papers, University of Iowa. Letter from Frederick to Marie Gilchrist, 8 December 1922; copy in Iowa collection. Printed postcard from Frederick to subscribers, 15 March 1920; Iowa collection.

17   Frederick notified his subscribers on 30 June 1920 that he had at last received the first issue and it was ready for mailing. (Printed postcard from Frederick to subscribers, Iowa collection.)

18   Edward J. O'Brien, ed., *The Best Short Stories of 1915* and the *Yearbook of the American Short Story* (Boston, 1916), p. 9; and *The Best Short Stories of 1916* (Boston, 1917), p. 5.

19   *Current Opinion* 67 (December 1919):330.

20   "What to Read," *New Republic* 18 (1 February, 1919):25.

21   In "The Aesthetics of Regionalism," which appeared in the January 1934 issue of *The American Review* (pp. 290-320), John Crowe Ransom wrote as follows: "Now a city of any sort removes men from direct contact with nature, and cannot quite constitute the staple or normal form of life for the citizens, so that city life is always something less than regional. But the cities of machine age are particularly debased. They spring up almost overnight, a Detroit, an Akron, a Los Angeles. They are without a history, and they are without a region, since the population is imported. . . ."

22   *First Chronicles*, p. 26.

23   There is some indication that Ansley's German descent was also a partial cause of his problems. Ansley, like Frederick at the time, felt that the U.S. should not enter the war against Germany.

24   Letter from Ansley to Jessup, 8 August 1917, in the Jessup papers at the University of Iowa.

25   Mott, in *A History of American Magazines: 1905-1930,* details the "periodicity" of *Midland* as follows (p. 179): monthly, 1915-17; bi-monthly, 1918-19; monthly, 1920-24 (combinations Jan.-Feb.-March 1920, Sept.-Oct. 1921, Aug.-Sept. 1922, June-July-Aug. 1923, June-July-Aug. 1924); semi-monthly, 1925 (combinations July, Aug.); monthly, 1926-27; bi-monthly, 1928—March-April 1931; monthly, May-Oct. 1931; bi-monthly, Nov.-Dec. 1931—Jan.-Feb. 1933; final combination number March-April, May-June 1933.

26   *A History of American Magazines, 1905-1930,* p. 186.

27   Letter from Walter Muilenburg to his brother, James, 14 August 1924, in the Iowa collection.

28   Roy Meyer, *The Middle Western Farm Novel in the Twentieth Century* (Lincoln, 1965), p. 83. See also pp. 84-87 and 212-13.

29   Letter from Frederick to Jessup, 7 February 1921, in the Jessup papers.

30   Letter from Hardin Craig to Jessup, 1 March 1921, in the Jessup papers.

31   *The Theory of American Literature* (Ithaca, 1965), p. 161.

32   See "American Literature in Colleges and Universities," *School and Society* 23 (6 March 1926):307-08. Also see "Teaching American Literature in American Colleges," *American Mercury* 13 (March 1928):328-30.

33   When Frederick went to Pittsburgh, Craig wrote Dean Kay arguing that Frederick be offered $3,500 ($1,000 more than his salary had been) to return to Iowa. See Letter from Craig to Dean Kay, 11 December 1922, in the Jessup papers. In "The Farm in Iowa Fiction," *Palimpsest* 32 (March 1951):50, Frederick wrote: "In 1922 I began to teach at the State University of Iowa what was, I believe, the first course in contemporary American literature ever offered at an American university."

34   H. L. Mencken, "The Literary Capital of the United States," *Nation* 27 (17 April 1920):91-92. The two exceptions Mencken referred to were Abraham Cahan, a New Yorker who had earlier founded the major Yiddish newspaper *Jewish Daily Forward,* and the Virginian James Branch Cabell.

35   Letter from Frederick to Mencken, 18 October, 1921, in the New York Public Library.

36   Mott, *"The Midland,"* Palimpsest 43 (March 1962):136.

37   *Ibid.,* p. 137.

38   A Ph.D. dissertation was written about Mott at the University of Missouri in 1968: "Frank Luther Mott: Journalism Educator," by Max L. Marshall. In the dissertation Mott's association with Frederick and *Midland* is covered briefly; biographical information here is taken largely from this source.

39   Mott, *Palimpsest* 43:137.

40   It is not clear when *Midland* resorted to printed rejection slips. It *is* clear that none were used for the first several years; in 1922 the editors wrote *"The Midland* has no rejection slip" (8.38). Frederick said he thought the editors first began using printed slips about 1927. The one rejection slip that has been located (now in the Iowa collection) has little sting in its first paragraph, no doubt partly because of what follows in its second paragraph:

> "This manuscript interests me and I appreciate the opportunity to consider it. It does not, however, quite fit in with my present plans for *The Midland.* I hope you have something else which you will care to offer me.
> "Just at present we are making a definite effort to secure new readers for the magazine. I am enclosing a circular which may interest you. I should be glad, indeed, if we might count you among our subscribers.
> Cordially yours."

41   Charles J. Finger, "The Midland Man," *All's Well* 7 (June 1927):7-8.

42   The first letter is from Frederick to John Beadle, 7 December 1932; and is owned by Beadle. The second is from Philip E. Stevenson to Mott, 6 March 1925; and is owned by Mildred Mott Wedel.

43   Letter from Leon Jenson, *Midland* editorial assistant, to Gilchrist, 7 January 1925; owned by Gilchrist.

44   Letter from Kantor to the author, 12 July 1971, in the Iowa collection.

45   Letter from Frederick to August Derleth, 13 April 1931; in the Wisconsin State Historical Society.

46   The existing manuscript records for 1931-33 are contained in the Notre Dame collection. Manuscripts were received during that period from Mari Sandoz, Paul Fatout, Roland Wolseley, Wallace Stegner, Mark Schorer, and others; Schorer sent Frederick stories at frequent, regular intervals throughout the period. The records show that after James T. Farrell's story was published in *Midland,* he continued to send stories to Frederick.

47   Wallace Stegner, "The Trail of the Hawkeye: Literature Where the Tall Corn Grows," *Saturday Review of Literature* 18 (30 July 1938):16.

48   Letter from Neihardt to the author, 24 January 1972; letter from Derleth to the author, 11 June 1971; letter from Benjamin Appel to the author, 15 June 1971; letter from Marquis Childs to the author, 7 July 1971; letter from James Hearst to the author 17 June 1971. (All are part of the Iowa collection.)

49   *Understanding Magazines* (Ames, Iowa, 1965), p. 315.

50   Bynner published in volumes 3, 4, 10 and 11 of *Midland.* In *The Fugitive Group: A Literary History* (Baton Rouge, 1959), Louise Cowan writes the following:

> "The Nashville poets knew their own work was as seriously executed as most of the current poetry being printed in America; but they might not have begun their own publication without Sidney Hirsch's urging. Hirsch was acquainted with a number of recognized writers, one of whom, Witter Bynner, in Nashville to speak at the Centennial Club, had come to a meeting at the Franks'. Impressed with the poetry he

heard there, Bynner predicted that an audience could be found for a publication by the group, which was made up now of Ransom, Davidson, Tate, Johnson, Stevenson, Curry, Frank, and Hirsch.

"Some time in March, 1922, Hirsch broached the idea of a magazine." (Pp. 43-44).

After *The Fugitive* began publication, Frederick and Davidson corresponded with each other (copies of letters are in Iowa collection). Davidson wrote about *Midland* in his weekly literary column "The Spyglass" in the *Nashville Tennessean,* 30 March 1924:

> "Our admiration centers on The Midland and Voices, out of the batch of magazines just arrived. Robert J. Harris' story, 'The Red Beard,' in the February Midland interested us more than most short stories. Read it, and have proved to you that a good story can be written on some other model than the well-worn machine-made, O. Henry model which magazine editors seem to think is alone suitable for American authors."

51   Correspondence from Smith to author, 26, August, 1971, in the Iowa collection.

52   Ezra Pound, "Small Magazines," *English Journal* 19 (November 1930):689.

53   The twelve sustaining subscribers recorded on the back covers of the 1919 issues were Mrs. Alice Weitz and James B. Weaver, Des Moines; Edwin Ford Piper, Iowa City; Hartley B. Alexander, Lincoln, Neb.; Nelson A. Crawford, Manhattan, Kan.; Mary Grove Chawner, Evanston, Ill.; O. R. Frederick and Alice Delight Ansley, Glennie, Mich.; Mrs. D. M. Halverson, Minneapolis; Marjorie Allen Seiffert and Florence Kilpatrick Mixter, Moline, Ill.; and Raymond Weeks, New York City. Half of these twelve were either editors or related to editors.

54   Letter from Frederick to H. G. Merriam, 4 May, 1928; at the University of Montana.

55   O'Brien, *Best Short Stories of 1930* (New York, 1930), pp. x-xi.

56   Letter from Frederick to Jessup, 28 January 1928; in the Jessup papers.

57   William Troy, "The Story of the Little Magazines: The Revolt in the Desert," *Bookman* 70 (January 1930):476.

58   *The Little Magazine,* p. 147.

59   Letter from Eiseley to author, 12 July 1971; in the Iowa collection.

60   The *Time* article appeared in the 12 October 1931 issue, pp. 49-51. Frederick notified his subscribers he could continue for another year in a letter to them on 16 November 1932; in the Iowa collection.

61   Copies of letters bearing on the merger arrangements are included in the Iowa collection. Also see *The Prairie Schooner Story,* pp. 142-45.

THE expatriate movement of the 1920s seems, in retrospect, so important that it overshadows anything else happening in American literature during that era. Almost all the writers of that time which we now read— T. S. Eliot, John Dos Passos, F. Scott Fitzgerald, E. E. Cummings, Ernest Hemingway, Hart Crane—were part of it. Yet in the 1920s, while the expatriate movement was taking place, American readers and critics were devoting much of their attention to authors who formed a kind of anti-expatriate movement, authors for whom the question of leaving this country was never serious or practical. Those writers were known as "regionalists," and the doctrine they espoused was generally referred to as "regionalism."

Regionalism was a source of much critical controversy during the 1920s and 1930s. In 1934, Henry Seidel Canby's influential *Saturday Review of Literature* published an editorial entitled "The Boom in Regionalism" and later featured as its lead article a debate, "Regionalism: Pro and Con."[1] Lewis Leary, in *Articles on American Literature from 1900-1950,* lists 320 critical articles on regionalism after 1915 by some of our most respected scholars: Bernard De Voto, Waldo Frank, Irving Howe, Jay Hubbell, Fred Lewis Pattee, Allen Tate, Charles C. Walcutt, Robert Penn Warren, Henry Nash Smith, George Jean Nathan, and John Crowe Ransom. One needs only to list some of the titles of these articles to see how emotional the subject could become: "The Fallacies of Regionalism," "New York versus America," "Anatomy of Provincialism," "Why Must There Be a Midwestern Literature?," "Regionalism: Cult or Culture?"

The controversy concerning regionalism was due, in part, to the historical ambiguity of the term. The word itself has been common in American criticism since at least the 1840s, but has stood for different things at different times in different places. Paul Stewart, in *The Prairie Schooner Story,* agrees that the term is protean: "It has been used to include the local color of Bret Harte and the objective description of John Muir, the sentimental humor of James Whitcomb Riley and the terse grimness of Mary Wilkins Freeman."[2]

Yet, during the 1920s and the 1930s, the meaning of the term began to crystallize, due largely to the leadership of the little magazines founded to promote regional writing: "In their pages, where regionalism was born and reared, lies the clearest revelation of the major issues involved in regional theory. . . ."[3] *Midland* is an especially appropriate place to look for such a revelation since it was the first and probably the most consistent in policy of all the twentieth-century regional magazines. The regionalism that emerged in Frederick's magazine was, of course, specifically a midwestern strain. But the issues that concerned Frederick and *Midland* were the issues that concerned most regional magazines and regional movements around the country.

New York:The Blind Giant

Midland's editorial position grew out of a fundamental belief in the diversity of the country. Throughout its history, the journal remained, as it said, "impressed with the variety of the American scene" (19.82). Because different areas of the country have different "ethnological, climatological, topographic" conditions, different kinds of societies result.[4] To be sure, the editors did not attempt to define the characteristics of these different societies or even to assign firm boundaries to the basic regions of the country, as social scientists were to do in the 1930s.[5] The *Midland* editors, however, did consistently use the term "Midwest" to cover the block of twelve northern states that lie between the Allegheny and the Rocky Mountains: Ohio, Indiana, Illinois, Michigan, Wisconsin, Minnesota, Iowa, Missouri, Kansas, Nebraska, and the Dakotas. They referred to this region as the "Great Valley" and spoke of its fertile soil and stable prosperity. Most important, the editors were convinced that the people of the Great Valley shared a particular consciousness: "We have found, too, that the Middle West possesses a regional consciousness. . . . The Middle West exists as a unit of life in the world" (1.32).

It is easy to understand why these believers in regional diversity viewed with such displeasure the increasing standardization of American life. This discontent is obvious, for example, in one of the few satiric short stories *Midland* published: "Drigsby's Universal Regulator," by Howard Mumford Jones, a frequent early contributor. The story pits Drigsby, the inventor of a contraption that would standardize the speed of a person's speech to 348 syllables per minute, against an over-worked professor. Drigsby admonishes:

Why, professor, what are we doing with all our industries: Efficiency—standardization! That's the word—standardization! Look at the automobile industry—standardized parts! Look at the packing industry—everything standardized. Look at any of our big manufacturing plants—look at the army—everything standardized—men, output, everything! (6.163)

In a fit of evangelical excitement Drigsby looks forward to the time when "every freshman in the United States will be turning over the same page of the same textbook at the same hour!" He feels there is not a "mite of difference" between "factories for turning out automobiles" and "colleges for turning out students." When the skeptical professor questions if this kind of standardization would not undermine a healthy individualism, Drigsby sets him straight: "Individualism is antiquated." If the *Midland* editors abhorred Drigsby and standardization in general, they especially abhorred the standardization of literature in America.

In his 1934 preface to *Exile's Return,* Malcolm Cowley pointed out that literary standardization in early twentieth-century America was due in large part to the fact that after the turn of the century "publishing, like finance and the theatre," became more and more centralized in New York.[6] It is no surprise that, from the beginning, *Midland* looked upon New York as its *bête noir* and viewed its own mission as one of challenging this eastern giant that remained blind to the real possibilities of American literature. Even when Frederick moved the magazine to Chicago late in its career, his justification was that from there he could better fight the domination of New York:

I believe that New York's literary despotism is bad: bad for criticism, because New York writers and critics know each other too well and see each other too often; bad for creative writing. . . . (16.370)

The editors usually expressed regret when anything gravitated toward New York, whether it was authors (even though many Chicago writers have drifted to New York, "it is not clear that New York has improved their work" [16.370]), or the action of a novel (the novel "loses power when Arrowsmith goes to New York—that from that point on it is less authentic, less racy, less alive" [11.181]). At times there was a self-righteous attitude about New York, as when Mott was solemnly "moved" to protest the comparison between Saki and O. Henry, in spite of the fact that "all the New York claque has taken it up" (17.76). At other times there was a mildly hostile note, as when Frederick referred to "the eager little writers for the New York book supplements" (15.50).

And once, there was even a suggestion of effeteness: "The challenge of the diverse literary materials in America is not likely to be heard by those closest to the tinkling teacups of literary New York. It will be answered, if at all, by others" (16.375).

The most frequent charge *Midland* made against the New York publishing world was that it was ruled by money. Frederick wrote that "the domination of commercial expedience in the literary world is to a large extent correlated with the centralization of editing and publishing in New York" (16.370). The commercialism there, the magazine warned, was especially infectious for young writers who soon learned to define success only in terms of publicity and sales. If a young writer hoped to be published in the big magazines, he unfortunately would learn to spin out his narratives to inordinate lengths in deference to the needs of the advertising pages:

> Many a Satevepost [*Saturday Evening Post*] story is written to fifteen thousand words in order that it may wind its final coils through the latest pronouncements as to soups, collars, and automobile tires. (14.214)

Even more damaging than the commercial standards of length were various other editorial requirements which the New York magazines and publishing houses demanded:

> The young writer who takes it as his aim to write sincerely and competently of American life as he knows it is met by the editorial demand that he distort characters, exaggerate situations, and develop a glib and blatant style. Otherwise, there is no place for his work. (16.369)

The journal cited a case in point. In 1921 Philip Stong, a young Iowa writer, published a story in *Midland* "marked by a rich sense of the atmosphere of an Iowa small town in mid-summer, and by honest and careful characterization." In 1932 a commercial publisher brought out Stong's *State Fair*—a novel later used by Hollywood three times. In a review of the novel, the editors regretted that it was a "trivial and somewhat tawdry" piece of work. The fair itself and the farm people were characterized by a "brisk smartness verging constantly on caricature." The journal's review ended by noting that Stong had no doubt formed his conclusions "as to what the public wants" (19.139).

   In short, *Midland* felt it was very difficult for any serious writer to break through "the barrier of commercial standardization of magazine publication" (18.1), without compromising his standards in the process.[7]

It was not only young writers who were being hurt by this situation. Because New Yorkers were choosing what would appear in print, the Middle West and the other regions of the country were being short-changed in our literature:

> A result has seemed to be a tendency to false emphasis, distortion, in literary interpretations. . . . New England or California or Scotland might have been less adequately and helpfully interpreted if London had selected all writings in English that were to appear in print. (6.1)

Esther Frederick lamented that even in travel books the poor reader was "dragged hither and yon" through strings of clichés about the Midwest ("gems of nature's architecture," "bonanza farms," and "innumerable creeks and rivulets meandering through rich pasturages"). The wise reader would do better to remain at home and see the Midwest "by way of railroad folders, government bulletins, and chamber of commerce pamphlets, from whose pages most of the books' illustrations are taken" (10.319).

To remedy this state of affairs, *Midland* prescribed the following advice: serious writers should remain in their native regions where they might develop their art unfettered by the standardizing and commercializing influences of New York. Their literature would be regional literature in that it would recognize and use "the peculiar materials of varied regions of the country, previously imperfectly expressed in literature" (6.93). It would express "the native, natural and genuine, not the remote, external, and artificial." [8]   This idea is basic to *Midland* thinking, and the words used to express it—"natural," "genuine," "external," and "artificial"—are key ones in *Midland* rhetoric. Good literature arises out of the life the writer knows best, which is the life of his region. As Frederick put it, writing and living must be "of one piece" (13.277).

Rural Stereotypes and Eastern Plots

ALTHOUGH the urbanization of much of the Middle West was well under way by 1915, *Midland* preferred literature with rural or small-town settings. This preference is obvious not only from the stories it printed but also from essays (e.g., "Can Agriculture Function in Literature?" [4.103]), and from editorial and book review comments (e.g.,

"Most Americans who have lived and worked upon the land will agree with me that this prospect [the depletion of the farm population] is not a happy one" [14.269]). The reason for this rural preference—for this shunning of the new, growing midwestern cities—had to do with two assumptions which underlay the thinking of *Midland*'s editors: (1) individuals and societies adapt only gradually to their natural environments, and (2) perfection consists in being assimilated into and being in harmony with the natural environment. These assumptions became most explicit in an essay-review by Mott, "Literature with Roots," in which he talked about the regionalists' "passion for the indigenous." One paragraph in the review is particularly central to *Midland* thought:

> There is much scurrying about the country in automobiles these days, and much accumulation of superficial ideas. The sophistication which is the goal of this kind of life is precisely the opposite of that true culture whose roots go deep into tradition and the ancient handiworks and the life of the race. These things root and grow in places. There is a kind of integrity of an old man who belongs to a certain environment and nowhere else that is not found in the cosmopolite who bears a dozen veneers one imposed on another: one feels that the old man with roots is more perfect and complete. And it is because of this integrity and perfection that all the materials belonging to unspoiled places in the United States are of the highest value for painting, sculpture, poetry, fiction, and all of the more fundamental arts. (19.82-83)

The journal's "passion for the indigenous" extended to the natural environment. An early essay, "Trees and the Homestead," recounted how closely man traditionally has been bound up with trees, which still shelter and nourish the farm dweller. A close awareness of the natural environment, the essayist wrote, can carry us back to the earliest state of human development: "The feel of the soil, the odors of the breeze, the crash of the storm, and the patter of rain drops on our shelter stir us because they bring back forgotten memories of the childhood of our race" (2.115). In the book review section, Frederick often admitted to being an unabashed lover of nature and frequently praised the work of two English nature writers, Henry Williamson and W. H. Hudson.[9]

The journal was concerned that midwestern rural life, in spite of its "integrity" and closeness to nature, had developed a highly negative literary image over the years. In much serious nineteenth-century fiction, the rural Midwest had been presented, as Henry F. May has pointed out, as a place primarily, though not exclusively, of "drabness, violence, and hardship."[10] William Dean Howells, sitting in Boston, had fostered what might be called a school of "pessimistic realism," made up of midwestern writers like Edward Eggleston, Hamlin Garland, Joseph Kirkland, and E. W. Howe. In the twentieth century, when *Vanity Fair* finally recognized the "existence, literarily speaking, of the region west of Jersey," it did so only by mocking the dreariness and drabness of what that eastern magazine called the "Sears-Roebuck school of fiction," where the heroes were all

> unsuccessful in business, poor in spirit, doomed to meet only the dreariest types of people in the dreariest towns listed in the postal guide. They . . . wear alpaca dusters in all love scenes, and sleeve supporters. (7.175)

When Sinclair Lewis's *Main Street* was published in 1920, *Midland* perfunctorily noted its importance. Later the journal regretted, however, that many post-*Main Street* writers assumed the population of small towns consisted of "stock characters" like "the ill-adjusted school teacher" and the "escaping youth" (16.126).

It was as if the midwestern small towns and farms were being constantly stereotyped in one way or another in literature, the editors felt. And the region was always short-changed in the process, for midwestern life was more hopeful, more challenging, and more colorful than any of the dreary stereotypes pictured it as being. Probably partly as a reaction to these stereotypes, *Midland* occasionally went out of its way to project a positive, pleasant attitude toward the rural Midwest. Frederick set the pace in the two novels he published in the twenties, both of which presented farm life as more interesting and satisfying than city life. In the journal he warned his audience against "the drabness of texture, the coldness and heaviness too often characteristic of American realism when it does attain honesty and seriousness of purpose" (18.64). And later he called attention to MacKinlay Kantor's novel, *Jaybird,* for in it Kantor brought out some of the "bright threads" in midwestern life:

> Some of us have been unjust to our material. We have seen only dull threads in a pattern which is really of exuberant variety and intensity of contrasts. (19.55)

Midland did not want a literary image—midwestern villages and farms as dull places, places from which to escape—to hinder native writers from seeing their region afresh.

The editors were also worried that preconceived notions of plot might come between a writer and his material. The authors of *The Little Mag-*

azine wrote that many eastern publishers in the *Midland* years demanded fiction with plots that followed a "mechanical formula":

> . . . obvious rising action, wherein virtue and refinement struggled on fairly even terms with crudity and immorality; obvious climax and denouement, wherein virtue and refinement victoriously subdued all evil. The happy ending with good triumphant was a necessity.[11]

The magazine was always wary of fiction having the marks of this formula, which it considered an artificial device to secure the interest of an undemanding mass audience. The editors condescendingly dismissed as a "typical summer novel," for instance, *Proof of the Pudding,* by the popular Indiana novelist, Meredith Nicholson:

> The heroine, a young girl who has been resuced from poverty and brought up in wealth and luxury, is at the opening of the story in danger of being spoiled by a fast society set that has taken her up. The manner in which her course is changed . . . is unreal. (2.295)

Later, when Frederick reviewed *Cuckoo,* by Douglas Goldrin, he noted that at the end of the novel "everybody is marrying everybody else, with Victorian thoroughness. Nobody is forgotten" (13.30). The terse last paragraph of that review suggests most succinctly what *Midland* thought about any book whose plot seemed as if it were inspired by a preconceived formula rather than by actual experience: "Anyone who wishes to read it may have my copy."

To compensate for the contrived, over-plotted popular fiction, *Midland* favored stories where the plot was so organic to the material that it did not call attention to itself and seem to be the most important element of the fiction. Zona Gale's Wisconsin stories, for example, were praised as "genuine," "natural," and "truthful," since she was never "hampered by any preconceived pattern of short story structure. She is not trying to force these authentic materials into artificial moulds of plot" (14.54). Once, at least figuratively, plot was even seen as something apart from the primary materials—something extra. Dorothy Canfield's *Raw Material* was favorably reviewed since she was "honestly interested in people rather than in plots or royalties." Even though her book consisted only of raw material out of which the reader, if he wished, might construct his own novel, "such bread alone tastes very good without butter and jam atop" (10.110).

If *Midland* did not want its writers to be overly concerned with plot, it wanted them to pay special attention to rendering a full, rich setting. Typically, reviews in the journal began with a discussion of a book's setting, and this matter might take up one half of the entire review. If a novel received only a sentence in passing, ordinarily the setting would be singled out for mention: "The backwoods of Ohio form the setting for William Dean Howells's new serial, *The Leatherwood God,* in *The Century"* (2.92). The reason for this emphasis on setting became most clear in Frederick's review of *A President is Born* by the prolific and then-famed author of *Imitation of Life,* the New York writer Fannie Hurst. The novel is set on a midwestern farm. Frederick admitted being moved to "mirth—to immoderate, irreverent, vulgar mirth" by the "extraordinary" nature of what he found there:

> It is a surprising middle western farm in that it has "stone hedges, most of them with their top row of boulders whitewashed. . . ." It is a farm where, coevally with the electrically lighted barns, the hay is cut with a scythe. It is a farm on which late in "the most backward spring of many a year," the sumach is "red as fire"; a well-managed farm, the admiration of the countryside, on which the lambs are born in October. . . . (14.157)

Inaccuracies of facts in the setting, he wrote, are not *necessarily* of consequence: "I have not forgotten who ascribed a seacoast to Bohemia." Yet, he continued, this particular novel is instructive because

> . . . Miss Hurst exaggerates the great sin of the mass of American popular fiction, of the stuff that fills magazines like *The Ladies' Home Journal:* fiction that masquerades as realism, borrowing its methods and its materials, but that actually is based on no adequate knowledge of the life presented, and proceeds from no vital comprehension of the men and women who live that life.

Mistakes in the setting in this novel are not "mere accidents of imaginative activity. They are the external evidences of the fundamental unsoundness of her work—its lack of valid motive and of authentic emotion."

Inaccuracies in the details of the setting generally were significant to *Midland* editors, then, because those inaccuracies suggested to them whether the work grew out of and reflected a vital comprehension of the life it was attempting to portray, or whether the author was writing about something external to his deepest experience. If the setting is incomplete or superficial, the characterization may well be incomplete or superficial. In Frederick's *A Handbook of Short Story Writing,* published by Knopf in 1924, he makes the point more forcefully:

> . . . human experience is always definitely related to physical environment, is actually influenced or determined by it. In transferring the experience, then, fullness of reality can be attained only by adequate inclusion of that physical environment.[12]

Anti-Local Color, Anti-Gentility,
And Anti-Romance

In its preference for rural and small-town literature and in its advice for writers to remain in their native regions, *Midland* was counter to the main currents of American literature during the late teens and twenties. Yet, in three important respects—in its anti-local color, anti-genteel, and anti-romantic stances—*Midland* was very much part of the mainstream.

The nineteenth-century local-color writers, such as Mary Elizabeth Wilkins Freeman, Joaquin Miller, and Mary Noailles Murfree, were surely the ancestors of the regionalists. Yet in *Midland,* this local-color heritage was referred to not at all, or slightingly, as when Mott praised B. A. Botkin for turning Southwest regionalism away from "mere local color, which often tends to superficiality of observation and feeling" (19.84). To understand the journal's disavowal, we must briefly consider the origins of the local-color movement following the Civil War.

In "Regionalism in American Literature,"[13] Benjamin T. Spencer states that after the Civil War—which Waldo Frank called the "death-spasm" of the sections—literature based on the life of a whole region subsided because writers were wary of calling attention to sectional biases that could enflame the old enmities. There were many calls, Spencer says, for literature based on one's more *immediate* surroundings, and many authors limited their scope to "small and politically impotent communities." Often this meant an individual village that was somehow different from those around it. In post-Civil War local-color writing, there was almost a premium on the idiosyncratic, the strange, and the bizarre; there was little impetus to focus on people, situations, or events characteristic of an entire region. This narrow, local-color focus, *Midland* felt, limited a writer and made what he had to say less truthful, less valuable. The magazine encouraged writers to portray the life representative of a whole people, a life ultimately determined by the geography of a region. Frederick once said that he thought a writer should concern himself with something smaller than the whole nation, but something larger than the confines of an individual and perhaps a-typical village.

A second tradition in American literature that *Midland* reacted against was the late-nineteenth-century cult of gentility. Several reviews in the magazine referred to an important critical work by John Macy, *The Spirit of American Literature,* first published in 1913. Macy observed that our literature was "on the whole idealistic, sweet, delicate, nicely finished. There is little of it which might not have appeared in the Youth's Companion. . . . Indeed, American books too seldom come to grips with the problems of life. . . ."[14] Macy did not use the term, but the kind of idealistic, sweet literature he was talking about came to be known as "genteel." When *Midland* began publication, Macy's charge was still generally true and especially true of the fiction printed by the mass-circulation magazines, such as *The Century* and *The Saturday Evening Post.*

In *After the Genteel Tradition,* Malcolm Cowley called the two primary characteristics of genteel fiction its high optimism and its divorce from everyday reality.[15] Two landmark works reflecting neither high optimism nor a divorce from everyday reality were published during *Midland*'s first two years. The journal singled out both for high praise. Frederick called Carl Sandburg's *Chicago Poems* "a unique and necessary document in the case against the dominant ideals of our generation," because the poems show us "facts, rather than a preachment based on facts" (2.192). And in defending Edgar Lee Masters's *Spoon River Anthology* against the charge of being too pessimistic, Frederick wrote: "If Mr. Masters has erred at all, it is not in over-emphasis of the sordid and unworthy sides of life, but rather in over-idealization, over-spiritualization, of his people" (1.239). The rationale for including what the editors called the "stern, undeniable facts of life" in our literature was stated best in a review of *Arlie Gelston,* a somewhat controversial novel about a small-town girl of dubious moral behavior. Characters like Arlie, the reviewer wrote, are important not only because they are part of the race, but also because they play a considerable part in human society:

If, however, you belong to that very large class of readers who prefer their sociology and their fiction, their thought and their *belles lettres,* in separate compartments—if, in other words, you turn to fiction merely as an escape from more exacting pursuits and a 'sublimation' of your desires—then you have no use for any of the modern realism. It does not belong to you. It belongs rather to those who find in it . . . some satisfaction of an insatiable curiosity about human life. . . . (10.57)

This *Midland* defense appeared in 1924, two decades after Frank

Norris's *The Responsibilities of the Novelist* and three decades after
Hamlin Garland's *Crumbling Idols* appeared.[16] Clearly, the journal was
not in the front rank of the attack against genteel literature, but it did
play its part in a later echelon of that attack. *Midland* never created a
national stir by defending a highly publicized, censored novel—as *The
Smart Set* did when it defended Dreiser's *The Genius*—but it did rec-
ommend Dreiser for those "suffering from a surplus of sugar in the
literary diet" (12.281). The journal never became involved in a court
case for printing "obscene" words and "unredeeming" stories—as *The
Little Review* did when it printed *Ulysses*—but it did print words still
taboo in the established press.[17]

Finally, *Midland* lent strong support to the general movement in
American literature toward realism and away from romance. William
Dean Howells, in his 1891 essay "Criticism and Fiction," sharply defined
the issue. He viewed contemporary literature with a morality play kind
of vision; the young Realist, fighting for the "simple, honest, and natural
grasshopper," was set against the Romancer, who continued to defend
the "self-devoted, adventureful, good old romantic card-board grasshopper."[18] *Midland* placed itself squarely on the side of Howells's young
realist in its opposition to writing that emphasized plot over character,
fictionality over reality, and the strange and far-away over the typical
and immediate:

> How foolish are we who make a great hue and cry after literary
> material, pursuing it into far corners of time and place and strange
> regions of the mind, when all the rich variety and significance of
> everyday life, our own life, lies at our hands. (13.277)

Whenever the terms "realistic" and "romantic" appeared in the magazine, they carried with them predictable connotations. It was a distinct
compliment, for example, when Mott wrote that *The Story of the 168th
Company* belonged to the "realistic rather than the romantic" literature
of war. "Its place is with Stephen Crane and Siegfried Sassoon," Mott
said, "rather than with Scott and Campbell" (12.142).

Yet this simplistic dichotomy is deceiving. In *Midland,* as in Howells,
the important distinction to keep in mind is the one between the rare,
serious writer of romance and the mass of romantic writers who exploit
the genre for commercial purposes. Howells wrote that he "would even
encourage" the writing of the "finer" kinds of romance: "Hawthorne,
the great master of the romance, had the insight and the power to create
it anew as a kind in fiction; though I am not sure that *The Scarlet Letter*
and the *Blithedale Romance* are not, strictly speaking, novels rather
than romances."[19] Similarly, *Midland* had no fight with the genuine,

serious writer who used the framework of romance. James Branch Cabell placed his novels in a mythical kingdom and included events that could not ever take place, but *Midland* consistently applauded his work. *Midland*'s ire was directed at the kind of romantic fiction that filled the pages of the large-circulation magazines such as *The Ladies' Home Journal,* and at the escapist work of the popular writers such as R. W. Chambers; both of these purveyors of romance, in fact, were included in a comical *Midland* prospectus for a "Bad Literature" course "designed to immunize the student to all the more important forms of bad writing now current in America" (7.62-63). Just as Howells earlier had used the term "romance" to disparage not Hawthorne but those whom he called the "effete" romancers of the nineteenth century, *Midland* used the term to disparage not Cabell but the commercial romancers of the twentieth. Their thinking on the issue is similar enough that Howells probably would have agreed with associate editor Nelson Crawford in his satiric appraisal of three of the most popular, romantic writers of *Midland*'s time:

> The reader of Harold Bell Wright sees himself a spouter of pious platitudes—or, worse, herself as the wife or sweetheart of the platitude-spouter. A slight advance perhaps is measured in the readers of Gene Stratton Porter. Here is the ideal of the hero who combines the adorable qualities of Douglas Fairbanks (exclusively in the movies) and St. Francis of Assisi. Then there are the kimono-clad readers of Robert W. Chambers. I have never seen any one read his hectic romances except in négligé, and my mind refuses to entertain the possibility of their being read otherwise. (9.69)

The Use of the Past

A 1925 essay in *Midland* which dealt with the historical novel asserted that the work of the then-popular Rafael Sabatini (who wrote more than forty historical novels, biographies, and plays and was called "the modern Dumas") was not really any improvement over the favorite nineteenth-century "historical" novel, *When Knighthood Was in Flower.* Both meant "cloak-and-sword melodrama, a few important historical incidents, a few great men dragged into the story by the hair, all combined to make a fairy-tale fit to kill an afternoon" (11.295). Both employed a "clap-trap romanticism which increases the heroism and the virtues of our forefathers directly in proportion to the length of time they have been dead." Even the most respected historical novelist of the time,

Winston Churchill, the essay argued, was interested in "sugar-coated history" rather than in recovering the specific American past.

In *Midland* thinking, a sin equal to sugar-coating or *mis*using our historical materials was not to use them at all—simply to let them be forgotten. Frederick criticized James Stevens, a compiler of Paul Bunyan stories, for this by way of a metaphor taken from his Michigan farm:

> James Stevens in his literary method reminds me a little of the work of the old-time logging crews in some corners of our farm, in the cut-over country above Saginaw. Where it was hard to get the logs out— in a cupped hollow or across a ridge from the skidway—the men left the felled trees to rot. Huge straight logs lie there yet today, so close together that they touch each other and one can walk for many rods without stepping on the ground—rotted and worthless now after forty years—memories of men who spoiled and wasted, in one way or another, more than they ever hauled out of the woods. (19.55)

What was true of James Stevens was true of American writers as a whole, the journal's editors thought. They regretted that the "permanent" literature of our Civil War was so slim, and they especially regretted that midwestern authors seemed oblivious to the rich, historical material in the midwestern past. One early essay stated that in the settling of the "Great Valley" there was ample material for "one of the great stories of all time."

> No such change on such a scale has ever before taken place in the world; none such can again take place while earth's continents hold their assigned forms, for there is no equal portion of the habitable glove left virgin. Is not this a theme to stir the imagination and rouse the spirit? (2.144)

The editors felt so strongly about this that they lost the moderation which typically characterized their tone. On more than one occasion Frederick spoke of the American westward movement as "the most dramatic event in human history":

> In its swiftness, its magnitude, and its probable effect on world history, the sweep of white settlers through the Appalachians, over the whole of the Great Valley and the basin of the Lakes, thru the Rockies and the Sierras to the Coast, all in little more than a century, seems to me not paralleled by any other of the great migrations of the peoples. (16.373)

What midwesterners should expect, the editors thought, was a "great work" having the importance of and assuming the proportions of myth, but based on their own historical past. Mott wrote that the setting of this work would be "the prairie, than which the Aegean Sea or any Miltonic sea or plain is not more epical" (7.320). And earlier, associate editor Roger Sergel wrote that such a work would contain places and deeds "more integral to your past than ever the events of the Aeneid were to the Romans or those of the Arthuriad to the Britons" (2.26).

These and other epic references appeared for the most part early in the journal's history. Appearing along with them, and later over-shadowing them, was the somewhat contradictory idea that it was un-realistic to expect a great, finished, mythic work to arise out of a region with only a scant literary past. Mott wrote that races, like individuals, depend so much on a ripened past that a great and varied literature is nearly impossible in a newly-established society (14.214). Gradually *Midland* shifted its emphasis and suggested that the job at hand for midwesterners was to unearth the rough ore out of which writers would later mine the truly valuable works, the ore out of which the final story of the settling of the Great Valley would emerge. Iowan Johnson Brig-ham wrote in the journal that as important as are "the achievements of the organ-voiced Miltons who create and people worlds," midwest-erners should not deny themselves the "humbler literary creations" possible at that time (1.272).

This notion of regional literature as a humble but necessary ground-work for later, more finished literature gradually became accepted both in *Midland* and in other regional forums around the country. A year after *Midland* ceased publication, Howard G. Merriam, writing in *The New Mexico Review,* formulated the idea into what became a frequently quoted definition of regional writing during the next two decades:

> I should like to have writers understand regionalism not as an ulti-mate in literature but as a first step, as the coming to close knowledge about the life of the region in which one lives as a first necessity for sound writing. . . . [20]

Implicit both in *Midland* and in Merriam's statement was the reali-zation that the early midwesterners did not count among their numbers many people skilled in the literary arts—as did the original settlers of New England. The nineteenth-century midwestern settlers, busy with protecting themselves and with turning the prairies into farmland, usually did not even take the time to write down the folk literature that was part of their experience. Therefore, it was the job of present mid-westerners to make a "first step" by resurrecting and recording the pre-literary or folk materials from their past. Pains should be taken to record those materials exactly and to avoid the practice of James Stevens, for example, who "prettied up the old [Paul Bunyan] stories, doctored and elaborated them, made them 'literary' " (19.55). Frederick praised a book bringing together "collections of riddles and folk remedies, a full-length account of a tent show, stories of magic and witchcraft" (17.159). And Mott, in probably the most favorable review he ever wrote for the magazine, called attention to *Folk-Say, A Regional Miscellany,* the annual anthology which brought together authentic folk materials of the nation and especially of the Southwest:

> Professor Botkin has performed a real service in this series, both for literature and for folklore. He has turned the spotlight on significant kinds of materials. He has spoken for regionalism of a profoundly important kind, has given others a forum to speak for it, and, best of all, has offered us three annual storehouses of samples of it. (19.84)

This affirmation of the value of folk materials is closely related to a strong democratic bias present in *Midland* from its beginning. In the journal's second year of publication, the editors wrote that "Good literature must be the reading of *the people,* and among *them* must be from generation to generation makers of good literature [*italics mine*]" (2.4). They once even spoke — somewhat boastfully — of their region as being "democracy incarnate" (2.2); they felt that part of their duty was to justify the promises of democracy by fostering the arts among all the people. If the great midwestern epic ever was completed, they thought, it would differ from all previous epics because it would be based on the specific past of a uniquely democratic region where "there were no artificial distinctions. A man stood or fell by his own merits, and weaklings perished, or returned to the eastern cities where there were niches for them. Manly qualities counted — of brain, heart, and mind — the one family tree as good as another" (8.316).

There was some justification for the pride the editors felt on this account. The Middle West, unlike New England, was not old enough to have developed a dominant aristocratic class based on tradition. Moreover, the economy of the Midwest, unlike that of the South, was such that the relative gap between rich and poor was not great. Frederick and the others behind the magazine knew of and much admired the pioneering historical work of Frederick Jackson Turner, who characterized the Middle West as holding deeply-rooted ideals of "equality, freedom of opportunity, faith in the common man."[21] Turner posited that even though the peculiar democracy of the midwestern frontier had passed away with the conditions that produced it, the democratic aspirations remained and were "held with passionate determination." Turner might well have used *Midland* as evidence for his point.

Experimentalism and the New Psychology

DURING the late teens and twenties there were scores of little magazines devoted to various kinds of literary experimentation. Some of their very names point up a conscious attempt to break radically from the past: *transition, Secession, Broom* (to sweep clean), *Blast* ("typography's closest approximation to dynamite"). *Midland* editors were aware that, for some writers, experimentation had proved fruitful. Yet, they were not in the vanguard in recognizing and sanctioning experimentation in literature. The clear thrust of their editorial policy, in fact, was to caution against its excesses:

> We may as well face the fact that experimentation tends to encourage the use of mere devices and tricks, fads, gloss, and oddity. Much as our Era of Experimentation has contributed of value to both poetry and fiction, it has certainly given us a greater mass of insincere and merely clever writing than has burdened American literature in any other period of its history. (11.303)

Although the poetic techniques of Sandburg and the form of Masters's *Spoon River Anthology* were implicitly approved in early *Midland* reviews, the magazine avoided sanctioning or even discussing free verse as such. And it was not until 1926 when the poems of H. D. were collected—eleven years after the 1915 imagist manifesto appeared in *Some Imagist Poets*—that imagism was even mentioned in the magazine. Even at this late point, *Midland* seemed to take pains to remain uncommitted in the critical fray. Mott wrote that although H. D. succeeded "almost miraculously in achieving poignance for her lines through methods chiefly imagistic," he preferred "to forget the shibboleths of the contemporary criticism of poetry, and to rejoice in the extraordinary delicate, clean, sharp effectiveness of the verses" (12.198). On the whole, *Midland* seemed to prefer the more traditional verse.

Midland's recognition of and sanction of experimentation by novelists was similarly spotty. James Joyce and Dorothy Richardson, for instance, were never reviewed. Ford Madox Ford was, and his experiments with point of view were analyzed and approved. But this kind of acceptance was rare; much more frequent was the cautionary note. If the editors hedged a small comment of praise for the contrapuntal poetic experiments of Conrad Aiken, they unequivocally condemned the "unintelligible *tours de force* of Mallarme" and called the "revolutionary" verse of the late twenties the "feeble attempt to attract attention of self-invited guests who have arrived too late" (16.127).

The journal's position here becomes more understandable when we remember that much of the experimentation of the time in both poetry and fiction grew out of an attempt by writers to express and to come to terms with the new, post-World War I world—suddenly fragmented, skeptical of old truths, increasingly urbanized. These phrases do not describe the world in which *Midland* was primarily interested; to put it bluntly, the concerns of T. S. Eliot, James Joyce, and Hart Crane were not generally the concerns of the rural and small-town midwesterner. While life in the smaller towns and on the farms of the region was changing, it was changing much less rapidly than life in the urban centers around the country and around the world. And it was much less susceptible to new customs, to new ways of thinking. Thus, *Midland* tended to look skeptically upon many of the phenomena that we think of today as characterizing the twenties. In a review of the work of Jay Sigmund, a frequent contributor to the journal who wrote about farm and village life, Sigmund was praised for rejecting the "merely ephemeral" and writing about "that which endures" (13.144). The reviewer envisioned someone in the far future discovering a bound volume of *Midland* and thinking that

> in spite of all these pictures of the twentieth century life which we have in cylinders, and which we throw on the screen in our institutions of learning during the history lesson hour, it would seem that the people in the 1920's did not spend all their time in kissing and hugging, in dashing about in automobiles and seducing young women, or in the giving of dinners and wine parties. For here are tales by Sigmund, which seem to indicate that there were workaday men then as now. . . . (13.144)

The point is clear enough: *Midland* cared little for "dashing around in automobiles"—the reviewer might well have had in mind *The Great Gatsby*—and for other things which characterized some of the more famous literature of the twenties. Instead, the journal encouraged its writers to portray things which the editors, at least, felt were more permanent—and literary experimentation was not so necessary for this.

In *Freudianism and the Literary Mind,* Frederick J. Hoffman pointed out that after World War I, the popularity of the work of Freud and other psychologists increased at a tremendous rate partly because it "served as a revoluntionary document; it pointed away from the past." [22] Eugene

Jolas's *transition*, which printed sections of *Finnegan's Wake* as *Work in Progress*, and other little magazines became forums for psychological fiction and criticism. *Midland*'s attitude toward what came to be called "the new psychology," like its attitude toward experimentation, was one of skepticism and caution.

In the few instances where *Midland* commented favorably on psychologically oriented critical works, a caveat always was included. Van Wyck Brooks's *The Pilgrimage of Henry James*, which takes a broadly psychological approach to biography, was called "one of the most brilliant pieces of literary criticism that has appeared in this country." But this, it was implied, was in spite of rather than because of Brooks's psychological propensities. In 1932 Mott reviewed at some length Ludwig Lewisohn's important critical work *Expression in America*, which uses Freudian analysis to attack the Puritan tradition. Mott liked the section on Emerson, but declared himself unfriendly toward the work as a whole because of Lewisohn's "belligerent championship of questionable attitudes and methods." Mott took special offense at the author's gratification in finding "long-dead men of letters in sexual aberrancies and abnormalities." Mott wrote incredulously that, as Lewisohn would have it,

> Emerson and Thoreau were 'chilled, under-sexed valetudinarians'; Wigglesworth's sex-suppression was sublimated in blood-thirstiness; the psychopathic Poe was 'hopelessly crippled in the most vital and pervasive of human functions by a trauma sustained in infancy'; Whitman was a pederast. (19.167)

Mott's fundamental disagreement was with Lewisohn's assumption that sex is "pervasive." In his review of Joseph Wood Krutch's biography of Poe, which also employs the "Freud-Jung theory of the subconscious," Mott was openly skeptical:

> It may well be that in another decade or two Freudianism may take its place with exploded pseudo-sciences like phrenology (which was once quite as widely accepted as the fantastic theories of Sigmund Freud now are). (12.300)

Midland's position here was due partly to the fact that during the twenties the new psychology became a fad in the worst sense. The original concepts of Freud became greatly watered-down and debased. The complex concepts of introversion and extroversion, which Jung had carefully developed and painstakingly qualified in *Psychological Types*, were turned into a popular American parlor game called "Know Your Type." The psychoanalytic jargon, according to Hoffman, became "part of the small change of popular journalism and was used to add a spurious scientific note to off-color stories about murders, divorces, and other newspaper fare."[23] Mass circulation magazines like *The Century* ran articles revealing the secrets of the psychoanalyst's couch. In short, there was money to be made by a young author if he chose to write for an audience hungry for this kind of material. *Midland* wished to discourage him from the temptation.

There was undoubtedly a second reason for *Midland*'s attitude, and this was more personal. In spite of the fact that the editors were working to move American literature away from its genteel, nineteenth-century moorings, they were respectable family men themselves who probably found the sexual orientation of much of the new psychology somewhat excessive.

Midland's Assessment of American Literature: The Past, the Southerners, and the Negroes

THE influential but short-lived *Seven Arts* magazine—published during 1916 and 1917, and edited by James Oppenheim, Waldo Frank, and Van Wyck Brooks—devoted almost half its space to critical articles which attempted to reassess American literature and American culture. Criticism was not *Midland*'s forte; long, critical articles were included only sporadically in its pages. Nevertheless, over the years, through occasional long reviews and many frequent shorter ones, a view of American literature did emerge in its pages. It is a view which seems somewhat strange to us today, but one that was completely consistent with the journal's over-all editorial policies.

As we would expect, the editors tended to consider earlier American literature as a series of discrete movements developing individually. Mott wrote that because of the variety and scope of the country, the "history of American literature is, in the main, a tissue of regional movements":

> From Captain Smith's *True Relation* as written by campfires of the James River, devoted to description of the Virgin Queen's new dominion, and Mather's *Magnalia,* rooted in New England as deeply as ever a book was rooted, we find all the older writers more or less strictly wedded to place. (19.83)

Then, according to Mott, came the Hudson River literature with Washington Irving and "a great New England movement" that included Nathaniel Hawthorne ("thoroughly a regionalist in all his work except that which was ill-inspired by his visit abroad late in life"). Other regional movements followed: a Southern one ("Longstreet, Baldwin and others"), a Western one ("Judge Hall, Davy Crockett, and Mrs. Kirkland"), a later and more realistic New England one ("Mrs. Stowe and Rose Terry"), and a later Southern one ("George W. Cable, Charles Egbert Craddock, Joel Chandler Harris"). One advantage to this regional approach was that the magazine was more attuned to little-known but excellent past writers who were somewhat aside from the orthodox path of literary study—writers like Ambrose Bierce, Thomas Chandler Haliburton, Lafcadio Hearn, E. W. Howe, and George Washington Cable.[24]

Of the major nineteenth-century novelists, the magazine's treatment of Henry James is most notable. In *Midland's* entire eighteen years of publication, there was never any mention of his work, and his name was mentioned only twice. One of these times was in the short review of Van Wyck Brooks's *The Pilgrimage of Henry James* (11.187) referred to above. The reviewer liked the work, but for him, this story of a man who left his own country had "much more pathos . . . than Hale's once famous story of a political expatriate." The review began with a hypothetical scene from "The Elysium of Authors" where writers are found talking about the kind of biographies then in vogue. The exchange between Mark Twain and James uses the former to satirize the latter; it represents in a nutshell *Midland's* attitude toward the man who wisely "went about the world seeing it always with Missouri eyes" (11.174) and toward the man who was not only without a region but who finally renounced his American citizenship:

> *Twain.* [talking to Maupassant]—Oh, you've been psyched too, have you? Well, so've I—psyched all to hell. What about you, James, old top?
> *James.* —I have not infrequently asked myself in an effort (or if it was not effort perhaps it was in any case a more or less definable attempt) to capture what might conceivably be my feeling or impression, though ever so slightly impacted from the supposition, if I should be as you say in your delightfully, although in the least degree coarsely, vulgar idiom 'psyched.' (11.187)

The bulk of critical comment in *Midland* dealt with contemporary midwestern authors. To a surprising degree, however, the editors followed two contemporary "tissues" of writing which were not midwestern and which have since been judged crucial to the full development of American literature.

The first of these movements was the one that was occurring in probably the most distinctive region of the country, the South. In commenting on Howard W. Odum's *An American Epic*—a work attempting to trace the southern temperament since the Civil War by using pictures, editorials from newspapers, fragments from magazines and books—Frederick spoke of the "tremendous challenge" the South held for writers. He thought Odum's particular attempt to meet this challenge lost some effectiveness because of its inclusiveness, and he suggested an alternative approach:

> I believe that he could have achieved equivalent truthfulness, however, with much greater interest and lasting effect, if he had found it possible to build his diverse materials into an organic fictional structure, based on the career of a single family. The result would have been such a novel as we have in *The Forsyte Saga* or *The Buddenbrooks*. No such novel of southern life has yet been written. . . . (16.375)

This statement, written in 1930, is historically ironic since it seems to call for an author precisely like William Faulkner, who had published *Soldiers Pay* in 1926 and both *Sartoris* and *The Sound and the Fury* in 1929. Frederick recently stated that probably both he and Mott, who between them wrote most *Midland* reviews in the thirties, had simply not gotten around to reading Faulkner until after the journal ceased publication in 1933. (It is true that Faulkner's early reputation was spotty, much of it based on his sensational 1931 novel *Sanctuary*.)

If *Midland* did not know of Faulkner and did not feel the challenge of the South was being fully met, it still paid close attention to the careers of a dozen or so Southern writers. A sampling of comments will suggest the almost uniform sympathy the journal accorded them:

—of Donald Davidson,

> The work of Donald Davidson, in the old *Fugitive* and elsewhere, has always impressed me as original and genuine. (14.53)

—of Elizabeth Madox Roberts,

> Miss Roberts is certainly one of the most interesting of contemporary American writers. Her highly individual and distinguished novel of Kentucky farm life, *The Time of Man*, was followed by a book considerably different, more introspective and somewhat experimental in method, *My Heart and Flesh*. (15.93-94)

—of DuBose Heyward,

> Altogether, I find *Skylines and Horizons* a profoundly satisfying

contribution to that American poetry of regions which is more than regional in its appeal and its significance. (10.423)

—of Ellen Glasgow,

Miss Glasgow [in *The Romantic Comedians*] shows herself a first-rate ironist; there is not a little Meredithean here. (13.96)

—of Thomas Wolfe,

It is a long time since I have been so much excited by any first novel, or any American novel, as I am by Thomas Wolfe's *Look Homeward, Angel* (Scribner, $2.50). . . . It is so richly poetic and so meaty with reality of character and experience that each page must be savored, thought over. (16.125)

The other non-midwestern, contemporary movement in which *Midland* showed a special interest was racial, rather than regional. The magazine's interest in literature by and about blacks started becoming especially noticeable when Mott was appointed coeditor in 1925, after just taking his degree at Columbia, where he had become interested in the Harlem writers. But as early as 1917, associate editor Nelson Crawford criticized the fact that black poets had "been narrowly Anglo-Saxon or else super-ficially—in matter of dialect and the like—African" (3.358). And one of Frederick's continuing enthusiasms was the work of Julia Peterkin, a white South Carolinian who wrote of the Gullah Negroes' everyday life. In one review of her work, Frederick credited her with being partly responsible for "the establishment of the Negro in his present place in American fiction: certainly the most dramatic event, and probably the most significant, in recent literary history" (15.92). Frederick went on to suggest that the place of the white writer in this dramatic event would continue to decrease in importance as the number of competent Negro interpreters increased. Mott, who wrote regular reviews of the work of Countee Cullen, W. E. B. DuBois, Langston Hughes, and Claude McKay, cautioned the Negro against imitation, against selling too cheaply his distinctive heritage for "the white man's mess of literary pottage":

It is bad counsel to advise the Negro to refrain from anything that smacks of propaganda, to throw away Negro dialect, to abandon the materials of Negro life—in short to forget he is a Negro. Abject imitation is the worst of literary sins; and for the Negro to be con-temptuous of his own materials and his own endowment is a sin not only against literature but against his race and against himself. (13.122)

The Midwestern Novelists of the Twenties

A surprisingly large number of the major American fiction writers of the twenties—Sherwood Anderson, Willa Cather, Theodore Dreiser, Sinclair Lewis, Ernest Hemingway, F. Scott Fitzgerald—grew up in the Middle West. The amount of attention these writers received in *Midland* seems almost directly related to the literary use they made of the region of their birth.

At one extreme is Fitzgerald, who grew up in Minneapolis but who left the Midwest for both his life and his literature; his novels are set at Princeton, on Long Island, along the Riviera, or in Hollywood. Fitzgerald's name does not appear anywhere in the twenty volumes of the journal. Hemingway, his fellow expatriate who set his work primarily in Europe, received only minimal attention. The brief *Midland* comments on *In Our Time,* in 1926, are revealing because they suggest that it was precisely the subject matter of Hemingway—the man who became the spokesman for the lost generation—which kept his literature from having real importance:

> Mr. Hemingway has a strong feeling for the realistic portrayal of experience; but the experiences he writes of do not always have much significance, and unfortunately he does not write well enough to lift his less important matter into the domain of literature. He is a writer of great promise, however, and in the two stories mentioned there is more than promise—there is achievement. (12.138)

According to the journal, no great promise was realized in *The Sun Also Rises,* briefly reviewed the following year. Yet the reviewer felt the novel was worth pondering because of its "profound comprehension of a contemporary attitude of mind" (13.184). When *A Farewell to Arms* came out in 1929, it was one of five books mentioned in "Some Novels of the Great War"[25] ; the treatment it received reflected, among other things, *Midland*'s disregard for national critical opinion:

> Of the new American novels about the war, probably the most discussed is Ernest Hemingway's *A Farewell to Arms* (Scribner, $2.50). It has been overpraised. It is neither so uniformly excellent in execution nor so philosophically profound as has been claimed. (15.277)

Sinclair Lewis, who put the Middle West firmly on the literary map with *Main Street* in 1920, was given more attention than Hemingway. His work was reviewed regularly, yet there was always an ambivalence about the reviews, a suggestion that Lewis *was* doing on a slightly higher level what the popular writers were doing: dealing in types. The editors observed in 1930, for instance, that Nard Jones's *Oregon Detour* contained "the stock characters of most regional novels since *Main Street*" (16.126).

Dreiser, who used midwestern materials sporadically throughout his career, received more sympathy in the journal. In a long review of *An American Tragedy,* Frederick declared that he had been a Dreiser fan since first reading *Sister Carrie,* had assigned Dreiser to his classes, had prescribed him to friends, and had even contested with "militant librarians" over the question of his moral influence (12.281). Yet Frederick found *An American Tragedy* "not the great American novel in more than a corporeal sense." In later considering Dreiser's *Dawn: An Autobiography of Early Youth,* Frederick succinctly and perceptively covered the worst and the best in Dreiser:

> There are repetitions, unconscionable detailings of the unimportant, ponderous and banal philosophizings. But these things are in all the novels, as well; and as in the novels, the essential substance of this book emerges from behind them with a strangely absorbing and overwhelming power. (18.64)

When *Midland* began publication, Willa Cather already had published her major novels dealing with rural midwestern life and was too successful a writer to appear in a magazine which, as a matter of principle, did not pay for stories. But were she not so successful, she might have been the journal's ideal contributor. In 1916 Frederick wrote that from her novels came "the truest interpretation of American life" (2.124). Later Mott said that her standing as an artist came from her ability to use "significant detail (as opposed to dramatic climaxes) and her faculty for the assimilation of character to natural setting" (12.140)—two things *Midland* always took as the sign of a good regionalist. There was no note of regret in the journal when Cather deserted her native region in two novels near the end of the twenties—*Death Comes for the Archbishop* and *Shadows on the Rock*—but there was obvious pleasure when she returned to a midwestern setting for her stories in *Obscure Destinies,* published in 1932. Of one story in that collection, "Neighbor Rosicky," Frederick wrote probably the most generous words he ever wrote in the magazine:

> I am almost afraid to say how much I like this story. It expresses for

me as definitely as anything I have read and as beautifully, the subtle
and profound relation between certain men and the earth. . . . (19.139)

Of all midwestern fiction writers, Sherwood Anderson received the
most attention in the magazine. Frederick, Mott, and associate editors
Nelson Crawford and George Carver each. attested to his importance.[26]
To be sure, there were some qualifications expressed about his work,
which is understandable given *Midland's* skeptical attitude toward the
new psychology and its value for literature. But Anderson did too many
things the editors admired for his general psychological orientation to
count very heavily against him. In one uncharacteristically long twelve-
page review by Crawford in 1922, Anderson was called "certainly the
most promising and original, if not the greatest, American writer of
fiction" (8.299). Anderson represented for the magazine, as Crawford
said, a midwestern author who could — unlike Lewis — move from the
relatively obscure pages of *The Little Review* in 1915 to the pages of
Vanity Fair in 1921 without altering his vision of the Midwest, without
tailoring his work in any way to suit the demands of commercialism.
Moreover, Anderson subscribed to *Midland's* notion that the most significant literature grows out of older, traditional societies; the magazine even reprinted part of Anderson's foreword to *Mid-American
Chants* as if to corroborate their point:

> To me it seems that song belongs with and has its birth in the memory
> of older things than we know. In the beaten paths of life, when many
> generations of men have walked the streets of a city or wandered at
> night in the hills of an old land, the singer arises. (8.303)

There is one additional reason the editors found Anderson easy to
like. His work, they thought, disproved the contention that there is any
conflict between regionalism and universality in art: "Anderson knows
what he calls Mid-America, but he also knows humanity" (8.301).

The Poets and Neihardt

OF all past American poets, *Midland* was interested almost exclusively
in Walt Whitman. As the following comments suggest, Whitman served
in the magazine as a kind of touchstone for modern poetry and prose
as well:

> As free verse, it [the *Spoon River Anthology*] belongs rather to the

pure succession of Whitman than with the sickening puerilities of most of our self-styled modernists. (1.240)

In certain of the best poems of the book, such as *Chicago,* the manner of Whitman is suggested, perhaps as much by kinship of thought as by the form. (2.189)

It [*A New Testament*] is Anderson himself, revealing himself as no American except Whitman has ever revealed himself before. (8.306)

One reason for Whitman's stature in *Midland* was that he represented to the editors a poet of the people who challenged the standards of the academy. In 1927 when Mott reviewed a critical work on Whitman by John Bailey, an Englishman with a classical education, Mott objected to Bailey's condescending tone in talking about Whitman and added that "a classical education would possibly have killed Whitman's magnificent originality" (13.31). And in 1931, when Harvard published a biography of Whitman, one detects in the *Midland* notice a kind of mirthful satisfaction: "Time does odd things to literary reputations. Here is a little book 'copyrighted by the President and Fellows of Harvard College' exalting a man who was once thought a vile and lewd fellow by nearly everybody in Cambridge" (17.79).

More important, probably, to Whitman's reputation in the journal was an idea that became explicit in a poem, "I Now, Walt Whitman," by Willard Wattles, a frequent early contributor. In the *Midland* poem, Whitman is supposed to be speaking twenty-five years after his death:

Here in the West, born of the sun and the prairie
Like myself in many things, tenderness, courage,
   devotion, knowing some things that I knew not,
Yet lacking in wisdom — humble, though, and yielding
   with perfect faith to my guidance,
(He himself could not say these things, but I can
   say them),
He I have chosen is setting in words not so resistless
   as mine were,
Still with a witness of earnest about them
My most undeniable message. (3.354)

Wattles felt that the deep emotion and natural rhythm of Whitman were passing into the twentieth century via the singers of the region Whitman himself had looked to when he had written "Pioneers! O Pioneers!"

O you youths, Western youths
So impatient, full of action, full of manly pride and
   friendship,

Plain I see you Western youths, see you tramping with
  the foremost,
        Pioneers! O Pioneers!

The criterion used to evaluate contemporary fiction writers in the journal was the same criterion used for contemporary poets: the attention received depended largely on the literary use they made of their native region. At one extreme of the spectrum—like Fitzgerald in prose—was T. S. Eliot, who was born and spent his childhood in St. Louis and who was himself an important editor and contributor in the little-magazine movement. Yet Eliot became a permanent expatriate who seemed to draw on everything for his poetry *but* the Middle West. His name never was mentioned in *Midland*.

The poets mentioned were the ones who wrote of midwestern life and who, unlike Eliot, were more clearly in the lineage of Whitman— poets like Carl Sandburg, Edgar Lee Masters, and Vachel Lindsay. Sandburg was praised for making a "permanent contribution to the literature of the Middle West and of America" with his authentic, realistic *Chicago Poems* (2.189). Frederick called Masters the "first great poet of the Middle West" because the *Spoon River Anthology* gave permanent literary form to the life of a midwestern community (1.243).[27] And Mott, in a 1929 review of Lindsay's *A Litany of Washington Street,* declared himself happy that Lindsay was not a "debunker":

> Mr. Lindsay, if one may be allowed the word, is openly and proudly and purposefully a "bunker." He believes, in other words, in building up and elaborating all the fine legendary materials we have (15.222).

Of all contemporary poets or fiction writers, the person who emerged in the journal as *the* major author of the era was John G. Neihardt. The journal devoted more space to him and talked about him more ecstatically than about any other single author. In the past few years there has been a revived interest in Neihardt's work, particularly in *Black Elk Speaks,* but almost no one would call him the major writer of the twenties. During the twenties Neihardt's reputation outside of *Midland* was perhaps even more limited than it is today. In 1925 Clement Wood's *Poets of America,* advertised as "the first complete and comprehensive survey to be made of the poets and the poetical product of the United States" (11.226), left him out completely. Mott called this "the great omission of the book" and soon was talking of "the growing circle of Neihardtians" (13.64).

Midland's interest in Neihardt was no doubt heightened by the fact that in 1915 he published some poems in the magazine and later came to know the editors well. Several years before Mott was associated with the journal, he read Neihardt's "The Song of Hugh Glass" and was so impressed that he got on a bus and went unannounced to Bancroft, Nebraska, to meet the author. This started a lifelong friendship between the two men. When Mott coedited *Midland,* he appeared together several times 'with Neihardt on the platform. Mott's diary entry for 30 November 1929, shows how they divided the work: "Read my negro poetry to convention — about 300. Neihardt preceded me, reading the death of Crazy Horse from Song of the Indian Wars." [28] In later years, when Mott headed the University of Missouri School of Journalism, Neihardt was a member of the Department of English there.

But none of this explains Neihardt's extraordinary reputation in the magazine. That is explained, largely, by the fact that the editors saw Neihardt as the person who was writing the great poetical work of the time in his five-cycle epic dealing with the settling of the Great Plains. Unlike many who had conceived American history "as entirely enacted on the Atlantic Coast" (2.25), Neihardt found abundant historical material in the Middle West. Unlike those who either "prettied up" our past or disregarded it entirely, Neihardt studied it assiduously in order to render it as it actually was. (After Neihardt decided to undertake his great work, he journeyed to the headwaters of the Missouri River and traveled 1,000 miles down it in an open boat in order to get a better glimpse of his setting.) Unlike most of our writers who had given lop- sided views of the American Indian as "a uniped, as the perfect man, as the red devil, a little higher than a beast, a child in need of a mission- ary, a beggar on a reservation" (13.156), Neihardt treated the Indians in- dividually and gave them the "sensible manhood and fine personality" that were theirs, even recognizing the real worth of their religion. (His credentials for writing about the Indians were very good, since he had lived among the Omaha tribe from 1901-1907.)

When the first cycle of Neihardt's epic was published in 1915, as- sociate editor Roger Sergel's comments were typical of the reception each successive cycle would receive in the magazine. Sergel hoped that Neihardt's songs would "take rank with, if not precedence over, Scott and Tennyson in our schools" because through them the "sturdy values" of the midwestern past would be passed on to future generations (2.25). *Midland's* feeling toward Neihardt was probably best summed up in a sentence that concluded a review in 1927 by Esther Frederick. The sentence may seem ironic to many today: "This is work that will last" (13.156).

Midland's Regionalism in Retrospect

SURELY the most significant plank in *Midland*'s policy was its challenge to the dominance of New York, its calling into question the standards by which many publishers there selected literature for print. *Midland,* of course, was not the only voice challenging New York's hegemony. During the twenties an article in *The New Republic,* for example, warned that the New York publishing world had become a fixed and hierarchic "self-centre"; and an article in the *Literary Digest* charged that New Yorkers were looking only for a "reflection of themselves."[29] Yet *Midland*'s part in this challenge was noteworthy because its warning—sounded from its very first issue in 1915—was voiced with such vigor and with such frequency.

The magazine constantly told the young writer from the Midwest and other regions that the relationship between good literature and popularity with the New York publishers was not necessarily a direct one. With regularity *Midland* reminded the serious writer that literature does not arise from artificial notions of character, preconceived patterns of plot, or commercial standards of taste, but only from life as the writer has honestly and sensitively perceived it.

The value of a subsequent plank in *Midland* policy, advising young writers to remain at home and to write only of their own region, is more debatable. In defense of their position the editors would have argued, as Oliver La Farge did in 1937, that the question of whether authors should aim for regional or general novels was academic: "In actual fact there have been very few stories written that are not fundamentally sectional with the exception of such panoramic works as Dos Passos's series."[30] The editors would further have argued that regional writing was just as valuable and as universal as any other kind of writing. As Frederick put it, "A good regional writer is a good writer who uses regional materials. . . . His work has literary importance only insofar as it meets the standards of good writing at all times and in all places."[31] Certainly, a regional focus helped to energize many American writers during and following the *Midland* years. In the autobiographical *Opinions of Oliver Allston,* Van Wyck Brooks, who has been called a "cultural nationalist,"[32] attests to this point by contrasting the "superficial" local-color focus of the late nineteenth century with the regional focus of the twentieth:

> Steinbeck's California, Faulkner's Mississippi, Farrell's Chicago Irish and the Georgia of Caldwell had served in every case as an admirable focus. . . . None of these novelists was concerned with the glorification of a region; nor did they point out the differences of their regions from others. They used the group not as a fetish but merely as a means by which to seek the universal.[33]

In spite of these points, the fact remains that by counseling the writer to remain in his region and also to be wary of literary experimentation, *Midland*'s policy might well have been stifling for some developing artists. One wonders, for instance, what might have become of Henry James had he been born in Illinois and taken this advice? Or of Eliot had he never left St. Louis?

An even more questionable part of *Midland* policy was its related preference for literature that depicted rural and small-town life. In effect, the magazine was betting on a kind of existence that was becoming less and less a major part of American life. The editors realized that the forces of urbanization, industrialization, and centralization were inevitable; they were not stupid men. Yet at least editorially, they never really came to terms with these phenomena. In this regard the policy of the journal was short-sighted or even anachronistic. Moreover, its assumption that the best literature arises out of the older, more settled societies simply was not upheld by the literary output of the era. Much of the best work of the time—one thinks here of Hart Crane and Fitzgerald—arose precisely out of the artist's response to an unsettled, rapidly changing postwar society.

All of these are serious charges. Yet there is an over-all consideration that is finally more important than a consideration of any specific *Midland* policy. This is the consideration of attitude—of the general spirit of the editorial advice. The real issue is whether *Midland* was "provincial" in the worst or in the best sense of the word. To use the terminology that the North Carolina sociologists Howard W. Odum and Harry E. Moore developed in their important 1938 work, *American Regionalism,* was *Midland*'s policy "sectional" or "regional"? "Sectional" thinking, according to Odum and Moore, is unhealthy both for individual areas of the country and for the country as a whole, since it is falsely predicated on "isolated, segregated areal divisions with potential completeness in themselves."[34] "Regional" thinking, on the other hand, is predicated on the sound assumption that the areas of the country are different yet component parts of an organic whole. For an artist, sectional thinking tends to promote an uncritical pride and a consequent narrowness of vision; regional thinking, on the other hand, fosters a healthy perspective about the real significance of one's material.

On this over-all consideration *Midland* comes out well; in Odum and Moore's terms the magazine was clearly regional rather than sectional in outlook. If the editors tended to stress the positive aspects of their region, their optimism was sensibly qualified and did not prevent them from occasionally publishing extremely pessimistic literature about midwestern rural life. If they once spoke of the Middle West as being "democracy incarnate," they quickly added that this democracy was an experiment, an aspiration, "not yet an achievement" (2.3-4). And the editorial pages never reflected the xenophobic tendencies which a sectional outlook would have engendered and which had been part of the earlier Populist movement in the Middle West.[35]

Indeed, the kind of literature *Midland* called for would tend to bring the various regions of the country together by increasing their understanding of one another. The editors were glad that regional literature would make Minnesota "a part of the experience of the dweller in New Orleans or New York" (15.93). And their frequent comments about literature from other regions reflected their desire to make those other regions better known to midwesterners. They kept in touch with the fledgling regional movements elsewhere through the exchange system and through correspondence. From the start they followed up these contacts editorially, as when in the first volume they noted a work of essays by "the enterprising people of the Far West" and called for similar efforts in "every part of the country" (1.278-79). They closely followed the careers of a dozen Southerners, paid special attention to the southwestern writers that Jay Hubbell and Henry Nash Smith were encouraging through their efforts with *The Southwest Review,* and devoted one entire issue to a group of Santa Fe authors.

The point here is that *Midland* was interested in encouraging authentic literature from areas that had been relatively silent — from the Middle West, from other regions of the country, and from minority racial groups. The journal early championed both Indian and Negro literature. In the late twenties Frederick made a prediction which, considering the Jewish and other ethnic literature of the present day, has proven incorrect only in one or two particulars:

> ... I regard the regional movement — the widespread recognition and use of the peculiar materials of varied regions of the country, previously imperfectly expressed in literature — as the most important and characteristic contribution to American letters of the past twenty-five years; and I believe that a somewhat comparable racial movement,

consisting in the literary expression of hitherto silent racial groups within our population, is likely to characterize the second quarter of the century. (15.93)

In short, although *Midland* was a midwestern magazine and always reflected its place of origin, it never did so with any sense of bigoted or narrow provincialism. The magazine's editorial advice would not have been particularly helpful to the established, gifted writer of the time, but he was not its prime target. Its advice was not directly responsible for any great works of literature, but they were not its primary goal. In some respects its policies were short-sighted, but in other respects— in challenging the dominant commercial standards of the time and in encouraging regional and racial literature—they were reasoned and perceptive. We may conclude with some certainty that *Midland*'s policies played a role, minor though it might have been, in bringing about a rich, varied literature in twentieth-century America.

NOTES

1   "The Boom in Regionalism," *Saturday Review of Literature* 10 (7 April 1934):606; "Regionalism: Pro and Con," *Saturday Review of Literature* 15 (28 November 1936):3-4, 14, 16.
2   *The Prairie Schooner Story* (Lincoln, 1955), p. 60.
3   *The Little Magazine* (Princeton, 1946), p. 128.
4   Note the similarity between this and the following from John Crowe Ransom's "The Aesthetics of Regionalism," in the *American Review,* January 1934, p. 295: "Coming to the theory, the first thing to observe is that nature itself is intensely localized or regional; and it is not difficult to imagine that the life people lead in one of the highly differentiated areas of the earth's surface is going to have its differences also."
5   The major work is by Howard W. Odum and Harry Estill Moore, *American Regionalism* (New York, 1938).
6   *Exile's Return* (New York, 1951), p. 4.
7   *Midland*'s analysis of this state of affairs seems corroborated by Hemingway's account of Fitzgerald in *A Moveable Feast* (New York, 1964): "He had told me at the Closerie des Lilas how he wrote what he thought were good stories, and which really were good stories for the *Post,* and then changed them for submission, knowing exactly how he must make the twists that made them into salable magazine stories" (p. 155). In this regard see, also, Robert Edson Lee's *From West to East* (Urbana, 1966). Lee's thesis is that western writers from Lewis and Clark to Bernard DeVoto altered their own experience to better suit eastern tastes.
8   John T. Frederick, "Culture of Communities," in *Community Life in a Democracy,* ed. F. C. Bingham (Chicago, 1942), p. 185.
9   Hudson is the subject of a recent book by John T. Frederick, *William Henry Hudson* (New York, 1972).
10   Henry F. May, *The End of American Innocence: 1912-1917* (New York, 1959), p. 95.
11   *The Little Magazine,* p. 131.
12   *A Handbook of Short Story Writing* (New York, 1924), p. 56.

13 Benjamin T. Spencer, "Regionalism in American Literature," in *Regionalism in America*, ed. Merrill Jensen (Madison, 1951), pp. 219-60.

14 *The Spirit of American Literature* (Garden City, N.Y., 1913), p. 11. In *Midland* (11.225-26), Macy is referred to, for example, in the reviews of Clement Wood's *Poets of America*.

15 "The Revolt Against Gentility," in *After the Genteel Tradition*, ed. Cowley (Carbondale, 1964), p. 12.

16 *Crumbling Idols* was first published in 1894; *The Responsibilities of the Novelist* was published posthumously in 1904.

17 Toward the end of its life, especially, *Midland* seemed to have few restrictions on the use of language. For example, in Harold Croghan's "Canvassers Neat Appearing" (17.117) the following phrases occur: "Those goddam stockings" (120), "you lousy little bastard" (123), and "You old bitch" (124). This story is also a good one to suggest how much more pessimistic things could become in *Midland* fiction compared to most commercial fiction of the time.

18 William Dean Howells, *Criticism and Fiction and Other Essays*, ed. Clara M. Kirk and Rudolph Kirk (New York, 1959), p. 13.

19 *Ibid.*, p. 56.

20 Howard G. Merriam, "Expressions of Northwest Life," *New Mexico Quarterly* 4 (May 1934):128.

21 Frederick Jackson Turner, *The Frontier in American History* (New York, 1920), p. 155.

22 Frederick J. Hoffman, *Freudianism and the Literary Mind* (Baton Rouge, 1957), p. 59.

23 Frederick J. Hoffman, *The Twenties* (New York, 1965), p. 233.

24 For Bierce, see 11:184; Haliburton, 11:163; Hearn, 10:420; Howe, 15:140; Cable, 15:140.

25 Others included in the review by Frederick are *The Case of Sergeant Grischa*, by Arnold Zweig; *All Quiet on the Western Front*, by Remarque; *Class of 1902*, by Ernst Glaeser, and *Overshadowed*, by Eugene Lohrke.

26 As Appendix 2 shows, there were eight different reviews of Anderson in *Midland*. The longest review appeared in 1922, four years before he became involved in the Iowa speaker controversy referred to in Part I.

27 *Midland* became increasingly unsympathetic toward Masters. In 1925 Frederick called *The New Spoon River* "undistinguished and insignificant," and noted that the original *Spoon River Anthology* appeared in *Ready's Mirror* ("of blessed memory!") while the new volume was "blazoned on the remunerative pages of *Vanity Fair*" (11.164).

28 From diary of Frank Luther Mott, 1926-1942; at the University of Missouri.

29 "Main Street in Fiction," *New Republic* 25 (12 January 1921):183. And "What the Middle West Resents," *Literary Digest* 64 (21 February 1920):35.

30 Oliver La Farge, "Heirs of the Pioneers," *Saturday Review of Literature* 15 (17 April 1937):5.

31 Frederick, introduction to *Out of the Midwest* (New York, 1944), p. xv.

32 See Claire Sacks, "The *Seven Arts* Critics: A Study of Cultural Nationalism in America 1910-1930" (Ph.D. diss., University of Wisconsin, 1955).

33 Van Wyck Brooks, *Opinions of Oliver Allston* (New York, 1941), p. 260.

34 *American Regionalism* (New York, 1938), p. 18, chapters 1 and 2.

35 In *The Age of Reform* (New York, 1955), Richard Hofstadter wrote that xenophobia was a common characteristic of the literature of the earlier midwestern-based Populist movement (pp. 72-73). There was little of this in *Midland*; if one excepts a few comments about New York critics, there was none.

III: THE LITERATURE

BETWEEN 1915 and 1933, years which cover probably the most brilliant period of the American short story and a time of major innovations in American poetry, *Midland* published more than 1,200 poems and nearly 400 short stories. Almost none of *Midland*'s poetry and only a small percentage of its prose would be considered brilliant. Yet the literature the journal published is of real significance to us because it represents the truest example of regional writing we have from the Midwest, if not from America, in the twentieth century.

Each story in the journal portrays its own unique world, but many of these "worlds" are so similar as to constitute a sort of collective *Midland* world. This collective world does not, of course, necessarily tell us anything about history or sociology, since it was only the creation of a certain group of writers. It does tell us something about what that group of writers was concerned with and, therefore, something about both our literary and our intellectual history.

What makes this *Midland* world particularly interesting today is that it differs so fundamentally from the world portrayed in the well-known, major short fiction of the time — fiction by Ernest Hemingway, Sherwood Anderson, F. Scott Fitzgerald, William Faulkner, and Katherine Anne Porter. The short fiction of these major writers has been comprehensively assessed by Austin M. Wright in *The American Short Story in the Twenties*. Wright uses Hemingway's story "Hills Like White Elephants" to demonstrate the most characteristic tendencies in that fiction.[1] Perhaps the best place to start in assessing *Midland* fiction is with a single story which seems representative of many others the journal printed: Ruth Suckow's "A Rural Community," published in July 1922.

The choice of "A Rural Community" is not haphazard. Frederick has stated that Ruth Suckow was exactly the kind of writer he hoped to discover when he launched *Midland,* and this particular story is typical of the fiction she published in the magazine. We might also note that the story's title suggests a calculated compromise between the farms and the small towns which the journal was most interested in portraying.

Technically, this story recalls earlier nineteenth-century stories in its fully explicit rendering of thoughts and feelings. But it resembles Hemingway's "Hills Like White Elephants" in its de-emphasis of plot. The narrative begins one autumn morning as a forty-year-old journalist gets off a train in the village of Walnut, Iowa. He walks to his foster parents' home, spends the day with them after an absence of many years, meets other relatives in the evening, and that night leaves the village on the outbound train. Nothing earthshaking occurs, and — as George J. Becker has written of modern realistic fiction in general — the author avoids any "neat denouement in which everything is tied up in a tinsel Christmas package."[2] We have, simply, the dipping into the stream of life of a midwestern village.

The visiting journalist is almost a combination of the two kinds of "migrant" figures Wright discerns in the major short fiction of the time.[3] His ambitious career reflects the American drive for success that is true for many of Fitzgerald's figures: he has worked his way through college and has climbed to the top of his profession. At the same time he has much in common with the expatriates who move around Europe and Mexico in stories by Hemingway and Porter; he is called a "confirmed wanderer" and thinks of himself "as a man without a home, or rather as a man capable of making a home in any café where he might chance to find a cosy seat" (8.224).

Yet he differs significantly from the more famous migrants. Like them, he has not been home for many years. Unlike them, he *does* go home, and after only a few hours there, his earlier world seems "to be melting away from him. He was all at once conscious of a void in the very center of his being." At two or three points in the story the reader begins to think that this confirmed wanderer may give up his life of international "flashing journeys." Although he does not, this possibility is raised, and it is raised largely because of the unexpectedly strong attraction the journalist feels for his family.

The Pervasive Family

In *Midland* fiction, when children get old enough to marry and begin families of their own, they typically remain near their parents, and their new families quickly become part of their older families.[4] In "A Rural Community," the journalist's stepfather proudly tells him, "Every Sunday

I got my girls and boys about me as if we's still all living together on the farm. Children and grandchildren and great-grandchildren all together."

A whole series of stories in the journal focuses on large family gatherings on special occasions, often a funeral. [5]   In one story a boy, who has returned from college for his grandfather's funeral, gazes spellbound at the casket and recalls the details of the old man's trip across the prairies when wolves and Indians were more than just memories. Suddenly, in the midst of all his relatives, the boy knows again "all the half-forgotten things, some of them gleaned from his grandfather's trip, some of them his own heritage from the vanished frontier" (16.280). This boy's family, like many other families in the magazine's fiction, is crucially important for its members because it serves as a repository for the values which members draw upon when they are together. An overly-serious character in another story puts it somewhat grandiloquently but succinctly:

> . . . where else may a man find verity if not on his own hearth, in the sacred sanctuary of the home? . . . And where shall he find the incentive to further endeavor and the maintenance of future ideals, if not in the fealty of those nearest him . . . ? (12.13-14)

Family gatherings usually take place in the "family home." In "A Rural Community," the journalist vividly recalls details of his childhood home even as he looks at the new one where his foster parents have moved lately. The details he recalls—it is built of rock, it has deep windows—rightly suggest that *Midland* homes often serve as a kind of extension of the *Midland* family.

This phenomenon is demonstrated in an extreme way by one of Hazel Hall's stories in the journal entitled, appropriately enough, "Home." This home is an old one that has been passed down through several generations. The symbolic details of its architecture emphasize the close relationship between setting and character to which the editors often called attention in reviews and essays:

> The interior, with its square, regularly-windowed rooms, its simple, inevitable furnishings, spoke through the unity of its design for the unified purposes of living, for the adherence to custom, for the putting away of all distant and disquiet influences. In its outer appearance the place was suggestive of enduring qualities not too rigorous to be insensible to the habits of change. (12.128)

At the time of the story five unmarried children live in the house. The oldest son had once been ready to marry until his fiancée astonished him by wanting to move into a house of their own. He had come to think of her only in terms of *the* house, almost as a decorative detail: "it was a delight to picture her seated sewing by the light of a tall, thinly curtained window." One sister had been in love with a man who had to live in a nearby city for business purposes. Since she "could not think of leaving her home and family," she married him with an

> understanding that she should remain at home where her husband would visit her as often as business interest permitted, until the time should come when she was willing to leave her family to make his home hers.

Of course, she never leaves. In this story the family is so much a part of the house that the house controls its very destiny.

The power of the house itself is not so strong in other stories, but the magnetic power of the family usually is. Running away from one's family is more ritualistic than substantive in the *Midland* world. Two stories are about boys who think of running away but decide not to; three others are about runaways who decide to return home.[6] One of these, "Prodigal," opens when a boy who has been away from home for four months awakens in a barn. (He had worked briefly in Chicago and then found odd jobs on farms.) The hay reminds him of his straw bed at home, and soon he is thinking about the odor of his mother's frying bacon. Before long he concludes it is "better to be a bond slave at home than to endure this empty freedom any longer" (18.70). The story ends with a brief, idyllic, homecoming scene; the entire family "sat before the fire" and "drank in with their own eyes the beauty of each other's faces." It is a "great festival"; no questions are asked and no resentment is shown.

This is characteristic in the journal: runaways are accepted back into the family, wayward members are forgiven.[7] In one story a Danish girl who works on a neighboring farm becomes pregnant by a farmhand. When the neighbor returns her to her own family she bursts out crying, but her father remains calm and stoical:

> "'It looks kind of bad, doesn't it, Martha? But we'll get through it, won't we?' That's all. I know that was all that was ever said to her. I could tell by the air of the house. It just went on being a good safe house. We went right on being members, one of the other." (17.161)

Almost always, families in *Midland* stories work out internal problems before they become severe. There are, of course, exceptions. One story ends with a mother beating a father over the head with a chair and their frightened daughter screaming to Jesus to intercede.[8] But this kind of situation is a rarity in the journal. Much more typical are stories where problems are somehow resolved within the family before they reach serious proportions. In another of Ruth Suckow's stories, "The Up-rooted" (8.83), the question of what to do with aging parents seems about to divide the children and their spouses. Just when things seem as if they are going to explode, the oldest son takes matters into his own hands and works out a solution acceptable, if not welcomed, by all. The family prevails. Its integrity—always more important than the integrity of its individual members—is maintained.

The typical *Midland* family prevails because it endures. It endures because it is predicated on a husband-wife relationship vastly more stable than the relationships one discovers in the major fiction of the time. This stable husband-wife relationship is in turn predicated on a somewhat peculiar notion of love that emerges again and again in the journal's stories. It emerges perhaps most vividly in a story whose title, "True Love," may at first mislead us.

The story is about two distinctly different kinds of love a girl experiences. She first falls in love with her college piano teacher, a would-be composer, when she is in his studio one sunny May afternoon playing Grieg's "Butterfly." The pianist kisses her, and their ensuing relationship is one of "pure joy"; like the ideal love of romantic poetry it is not hampered by thoughts of marriage or the future. The next fall, while he is on a Glee Club tour, she finds out—as has been half-suspected—that she has tuberculosis and must go to a Colorado sanitarium if she hopes to ever regain her health. When the pianist finds her note breaking off their relationship, his sensibilities take hold. He imagines that the disease "went over her like a fog, blotting out her sunshine" (8.208). This "fancy" pleases him. Caught up in emotion, he writes a poignant sonata entitled "Death in Youth," which eventually becomes a critical success. Meanwhile the girl slowly recovers. An older doctor who had diagnosed her condition, the "most dependable" man she has known, travels to Colorado and asks her to marry him. Although both she and the doctor know she still has romantic feelings for the pianist, she accepts the proposal; the "call for a home" is an overriding factor. Years later when she is forty, happily married, and the mother of two children, her husband takes her to hear the now-famous pianist play "Death in Youth" at a Denver concert. While walking home after the performance, the doctor asks her if she thinks the pianist is still in love with her. She replies: "He is still in love—with his dead sweetheart." The pianist, unknowingly walking behind them, sees them enter their home: "'Married!' he thought. 'Ye gods!' and strolled on, lost in his sonata, satisfied, bored, lonely, and rich."

The early love between the girl and the pianist is a matter of the heart. It is based on a "fancy," on a widespread idea of what love ought to be like. It is the kind of love one always finds in sentimental fiction and is related to the kind of love Wright finds in the major short fiction of the twenties—i.e., a matter of "feeling and impulse." [9] In *Midland* fiction, generally, as in this story, it is clearly not "true love."

True love in *Midland* terms is a most practical matter and tends to follow rather than precede marriage. Characters in the journal's fiction sometimes marry for extremely unromantic reasons: in one story, a girl's German parents arrange for her to marry an eligible bachelor nearby whom she hardly knows. In another story a boy decides to marry after his father puts things realistically indeed: "Got to have a wife to run a farm!" [10] Love, as it is primarily portrayed in the journal, develops between a husband and a wife over many years of living, working, and raising a family together. In this sense, it is more social than it is personal.

Wright finds that sex outside of marriage is a factor in fully one-third of the major short stories of the twenties; [11] illicit sexual relationships occur much less frequently in *Midland,* as we should expect. The few characters who do have sexual relationships before marraige are portrayed as selfish or ridiculously immature. [12] Adultery in the journal's stories is even rarer. One story where adultery is at issue is especially telling; it concerns a Montana rancher who thinks his wife is meeting a visiting homesteader in the barn late one night:

> John Wenger thought it all out, in his strong, unemotional way, standing there bare-legged before the open bed-room window. These things happened — were bound to happen. (12.227)

Cold practicality rules. Since he concludes that his wife is too sensible to leave him and break up the family, he decides to simply forget the incident. Actually, the marriage is never really threatened. We later learn that the wife was only taking the homesteader some medicine.

In his survey of the major fiction of the time, Wright finds a world filled with characters who are alienated from one another and who fruitlessly search to find a proper niche for themselves.

> The world of the American twenties . . . is fragmented both socially and morally, with each man isolated, obliged to find or make for himself his appropriate place in society and the appropriate principles to guide him. Almost never does one find a satisfactory solution. [13]

Midland characters do find appropriate places for themselves and appropriate principles to guide them. This is possible for them because the world in which they operate is more stable and more coherent than the world of the major fiction. It is a world dominated by the family, an institution based on a notion of love that clearly emphasizes pragmatic longevity over romantic totality.

The Old vs. the Young

In his book on *The Twenties,* Frederick J. Hoffman devotes an entire section to "The Very Young." He shows that Ben Hecht, Floyd Dell, Carl Van Vechten, John Dos Passos, and even Stephen Vincent Benét followed the lead of F. Scott Fitzgerald in exploring "every conceivable issue, trait, dilemma" of the young.[14] Wright finds that in the short fiction youthful protagonists are numerically more common than in earlier short fiction and thinks that

> the change may be broader than this. One notices in Fitzgerald's world, for example, how important youthful values have become as criteria for membership in the fashionable classes. Sports, so important in Hemingway's world, suggest the dominance of youth in that society. . . . [15]

Although the returning journalist in the *Midland* story with which we began our discussion is not young in Fitzgerald's terms—he is forty— he represents the younger generation in that story. The narrator stays with him throughout the narrative. Yet the journalist is less a character in his own right than he is a device to allow the narrator to portray the life of the older people. This pattern is typical in the magazine because *Midland* fiction, in sharp contrast to the major fiction, was generally more concerned with the old people than it was with the young.

One occasionally finds in the journal the same basic situations that one finds in the well-known fiction of the contemporary major writers— the rich young girl being courted (Fitzgerald), the sensitive person growing up in a small town (Sherwood Anderson), the boy returning home after the war (Hemingway). But in the *Midland* stories the point of view and therefore the entire emphasis is apt to be different: we see things from the parents' perspective, and it is they, rather than their sons or daughters, who are the real protagonists.

In Fitzgerald's "The Ice Palace," for instance, we know nothing about the parents of Salley Carrol Happer, the beautiful Georgia girl who goes North to meet her fiancé's family. It is almost as if she, like Jay Gatsby, has sprung parentless from a conception of herself. In "Wie Eine Blume," a *Midland* story about a girl who likewise is rich, is eighteen, and has been rushed by "the biggest catch in New York," things are very different. (It is significant that neither this girl nor any other girl in the journal's fiction would qualify as a bona fide flapper: this one is not quite lovely enough and her family is Jewish.) The *Midland* story opens as the girl comes home very late one night. We do not learn where she has been or what she is thinking, but only her father's thoughts as he lies in bed worrying about her:

> His mind slid away from the thin body lying between the sheets in the next room, but the thought took words. Is she a virgin? He did not know anything about her. (12.27)

The next evening her boyfriend calls and, we surmise, breaks off their affair. Afterwards as she gazes out the parlor window, we sense how depressed she is, but our ideas about her remain incomplete. We do know, however, how her father feels as he comes into the parlor and perceives the situation. The closing paragraph, like the rest of the story, tells us more about him than it does about his daughter: "He felt such pity for her that he could not speak. Besides, there was nothing to say. He stood aside when she walked from the room; it was all he could do."

Some of the most memorable characters in American fiction of the twenties are young, would-be artists trapped in the stifling environment of a small town. In *The Twenties*, Hoffman cites George Willard in Sherwood Anderson's *Winesburg, Ohio,* Felix Fay in Floyd Dell's *Moon-Calf,* Gareth Jones in Carl Van Vechten's *The Tattooed Countess,* and others. This same kind of character is the title figure in a *Midland* story, "The Poet." As an introverted and lonely boy, he begins to write poetry. In college, he does not mix with other students nor pay much attention to his studies. He drops out of school and returns home to work for his father, a carpenter, so that he can make enough money to write. Then, just after a publisher has recognized the quality of his work, he is killed in an automobile accident. The interesting thing here is that all of this is narrated completely by his father. At one point the old man had asked his son to explain his poetry to him. He recalls that after the boy told him he didn't think he could, "I stopped reading it. If the man writing it couldn't tell how it worked, I argued to myself, how could anyone else be expected to tell anything about it" (10.52). The portrait is less of the artist than it is of the artist's father in his attempt — with his limited background and ideas — to understand his son.

We can see an even clearer example of this common switch in emphasis in a story Mott wrote for the journal in 1924, "The Freight Whistles In." The situation is one that Hemingway uses in several of his stories, for example, "Soldier's Home." When World War I begins, a boy bored with life in his small town enlists in the army. On being discharged, he decides not to return to his hometown where his mother still lives but instead tramps on the freights. In Mott's story we learn of all this through his mother's comments to a meddling townswoman:

> "Tommy has a perfect right to see the world a little. He always wanted to. And I wanted him to, Mis' Shultz. You know yourself there's more interesting places than this town. I know you'll think it's awful, but I'm *glad* he's had a chance to get away. . . . You can see for yourself it would be awful dull to him here after New York and London and Paris and such-like big cities. . . ." (10.85)

The mother is the most perceptive person in the story, easily more so than the son, who briefly enters the narrative later. If anyone is to be pitied in the story, it is not she. Characteristically in the journal, old people not only dominate the fiction, but they are usually more intelligent, more interesting, smarter than the young. To be sure, there are included occasional stories about elderly people who lead dull, dreary lives.[16] But typically in the journal it is the sons and daughters who are the more pitiful. One is hard put to think of a single major character in the more famous contemporary fiction who is over seventy. But in *Midland*—which in this regard looks forward to Faulkner—the most memorable characters are grandparents, or even great-grandparents. From a whole gallery of such portraits, one example, taken from a story by the Wisconsin regional writer August Derleth, will suffice here to make the point.

In Derleth's "Geese Flying South" we have not two, but three generations represented: the youthful narrator, his older aunt, and his very old grandparents. The aunt, who lives with the grandparents, has called in the relatives because "something would have to be done about grandmother, who was losing her faculties, losing her mind, Aunt Cella said candidly" (20.37). When everyone is together the aunt waits nervously for the old people to go to bed so that the rest of the family can discuss the matter. The grandparents defy the group by staying up "looking at each other and smiling," ignoring the rest. Finally the grandmother says she hears geese. The suspecting aunt nods significantly to the others and says:

> "Now Ma, if you hear anythin, it's probably a dog barking somewhere."
> My grandmother looked at Aunt Cella and smiled. Then she said with a very detached air, "No, they're geese. I've heard them often enough before. I can't imagine anyone mistaking a dog's barking for the honking of geese." (20.37)

The aunt is amazed when she goes outside and actually sees the geese.

When she comes in, the old woman speaks to her "as if she were a little child," and further confounds the family by announcing that the geese are flying in a small circle — she has deduced that if they were flying in a large circle they would have spotted the river nearby and gone on their way. Everyone, including the narrator, soon feels "rather foolish." An uncle, anxious to get home, checks his watch and only half-jokingly observes the late hours the old people keep. Faces fall when the old woman proudly replies, "I remember once your Pa and I stayed up for two nights in a row and weren't tired enough to speak of the third night. That was at the World's Fair in Chicago, I guess." When one relative finally does leave, the grandfather suggests he take the aunt along with him for a vacation: "She needs a rest. . . . A week in Milwaukee would do her good."

Someone is in need of rehabilitation, but it is not the old woman or her husband. They have a knowledge and a cunning based on long experience that younger people necessarily lack. In the world of *Midland* fiction where there is a premium on mastering a known world rather than on charting a new one, this experience usually makes the old people more important and more engaging than the young.

The City Story and the Country Story

FEWER than one in eight *Midland* stories has a recognizably urban setting. [17] This proportionally small number reflects both the magazine's editorial position that the best literature grows out of the more stable rural areas and Frederick's personal notion that the urban areas were receiving literary attention out of proportion to their importance. The first thing one notices about *Midland* stories which do have urban settings is that they tend to be about people who suffer from a malaise, people who do their work with less vigor and less sense of accomplishment than the people who inhabit the farms and villages of the journal's fiction. The protagonist of the longest and one of the best "urban" stories in the magazine, the manager of a movie theatre in the Chicago Loop, is characteristic here.

The story, "Cinemania," begins when the manager arrives at work one morning and ends when he closes the theatre late that evening. The theatre he manages is large enough to have a staff of twenty-four ushers; in some ways it serves as a microcosm for the city. During the day thousands of people are guided around the enormous theatre in an orderly fashion. Individually they achieve some degree of comfort from watching the show and from just being in the magnificent place (the "Byzantine" theatre is built "in the grand style").

This order and comfort, though, are at least partly an illusion. Underneath lies near desperation. When the manager arrives at the theatre forty-five minutes before the ticket window opens, there are already hundreds of people lined up; "mostly, he supposed, it was to avoid doing something else" (19.9). At the front of the line are members of the Lou Montrose Club who will stay at the theatre all day wriggling in their seats with "orgiastic ecstasy" whenever their idol, who leads the orchestra and sings, is on stage. Throughout the day the manager must deal with a series of other patrons: a man who "accidentally" feels the leg of another man's wife, a big-boned woman who passes out from drunkenness, a lady who threatens to have him fired because there are bird droppings in one of the theatre's bird cages, a man who pretends to faint to get into the theatre free, and a prostitute who is soliciting the ushers. These people grate increasingly on his nerves. What causes him more anxiety is the fact that even though he manages the theatre, he is only a tiny part of a huge operation he does not understand. People higher in the organization than he — the Byzantine is part of a chain — are displeased with him because attendance, over which he has virtually no control, has fallen off. As the story ends, he leaves the theatre in disgust, knowing he probably will be fired in the morning.

The general discomfort of the manager both results from and reflects the discomfort of the theatre or, in larger terms, the city. In another urban story, published in 1916, life in the city is specifically contrasted to life in the country. A young Chicago waitress has left her Illinois farm because everything "was hopelessly dull and stupid" there, and life seemed like "a routine of work." She finds that urban life is a good deal different from what she expected. On the day of the story her first customer is a demanding, obnoxious man; her second is a lonely, pathetic boy; and her third is a ridiculous flirt who disgusts her. She begins to think that life in the city has a dullness all its own:

It was the same thing every day; one day was exactly like any other, scarcely varying in a single detail. The same hurrying waitresses in the black dresses and white collars and cuffs; the same orders; the same sort of customers; the same deafening racket; the strong smells and the bad air and the rumble of the city outside — that's all there was the whole day long. She had thought country life was monotonous, but life in the city was just as monotonous. Everybody was thinking only of himself. . . . (2.306)

As the people in the restaurant hurry through their meals, she recalls the leisurely discussions during the quiet meals on the farm. She has an inspiration to try placing an order to the back room politely. When she does, the only person who ever hears her amid the din—the cook—laughs at her.

Like many characters in the major fiction of the time, *Midland* characters go to the city to find excitement. The kind of work *Midland* characters usually find does not pay much, their lives become routine, they feel little control over their destinies, and the lives they fled begin to seem more appealing. No wonder that for some of these people the common pattern in the national fiction ("the progress is almost invariably eastward, to New York or Paris if possible, to Chicago at least")[18] is reversed. One *Midland* character, for instance, leaves a small town for a city where he becomes a stock clerk. When he moves on after a few months, it is not to a larger city but to the suburbs where he finds work as a gardener. After a few months in the suburbs, he moves back to the small town where he began. [19]

When characters do not complete the circle and return to their place of origin there is often, at least, a noticeable pull in that direction. In "The Visit" an older, successful California businessman returns to his midwestern farm to settle some affairs. As he starts to plough a field the attraction of the old way of life comes back to him:

> This was glorious. This was getting back at things! This was happiness! What farmer could ever escape his longing for the land, for the touch and smell of it, for the sounds of it, for the vision of it all laid out in soft ridges and planted ready to yield! (11.273)

His attraction here is specifically for the land. With other characters the attraction is for other things—the more rural concepts of the family and marriage, the importance rather than the obsolescence of older people.

All these things tend to make rural life more *stable,* and it is through images of motion that the difference between urban and rural life is frequently expressed in stories in the journal. In one series of brief prose sketches about "Any Young Man" in Chicago, the people there are described as "—up and down. Their lives are caught in revolving doors—snatched back and forth" (11.347). In the Chicago market the young man observes the "heaving and smashing, the pushing and plunging." In another story the haphazard nature of urban motion is emphasized: "His mind was full of a world rocking and falling and transforming itself into something undreamed of before—of new inventions, changing empires, a tottering social order, revolution" (8.218). In contrast to this, movement in the rural communities tends to be slow, orderly, as repetitive as the seasons. One story begins with an explicit contrast between the "far off" world which "rumbled and clamored" and the world where "life grew evenly." In this world of the farmer, men

> moved to and from the fields with deliberate, almost mechanical foot-steps. . . . Young men and women married, children were born, death came. Each left but a faint ripple on the stream of that life. (10.140)

In most *Midland* fiction men walk rather than ride the streetcar, and their work is tied to the cyclical pattern of nature rather than to the linear pattern of an organization chart. Most of the journal's writers seemed to realize that the calmer motion of farmlife carried with it the danger of dullness. Yet they felt that, especially in a world of unpredictable change, the slower, more repetitive pace had an abiding appeal.

The rural orientation also allowed *Midland* writers to express what was, for some, almost an obsession: their preoccupation with nature. In the story with which we began our discussion, after the journalist gets off the train he glances beyond the houses and sees a line of low hills. He stops, feels a "strange impulse," takes off his cap, and surveys the scene more thoroughly. The author's description of what he sees suggests the warmth of a Constable painting:

> Low rolling hills, fold after fold, smooth brown and autumnal, some plowed to soft earth-color, some set with corn stalks of pale tarnished gold. Along the farther ones, the woods lay like a colored cloud, brown, russet, red and purple-tinged. (8.220)

That evening just before the journalist gets back on the train, he pauses again to look at the dark pastures beyond a row of willow trees: "They widened slowly into the open country which lay silent, significant, motion-less, immense, under the stars, with its sense of something abiding. To come back to it was to touch the core of things." If hills and country-side seem momentarily important for this visitor who considers his home "any café where he might chance to find a cosy seat," they are almost continuously important for the people who actually live in the rural communities and on the farms of *Midland* fiction.

Father Leo Ward, one of the most prolific contributors to the journal, specialized in relatively plotless sketches that content themselves with describing some minute aspect of nature (e.g., "Black-Purple in the Corn," or "Rust in the Wheat"). In fact Father Ward, like the chief character in his story, "The Rain," sometimes was concerned with nature almost to the exclusion of people. In "The Rain" a farmer is painting the inside of his house while it storms outside. As his brush mechanically

moves, he keeps thinking about the crops, the soil, and the rain outside
on which he keeps a constant watch and which is vividly described in
all its phases: "great sheets of water swooped and bellied slantingly out
of a sky he could nowhere see, flinging themselves headlong over the
tree and the barn and the blurred grayness of the land beyond" (16.118).
During dinner his wife's voice drones on about wallpaper but he does
not hear it; his mind has never left the world on the other side of the
window.

It is easy to understand why nature is so frequently on the mind of
Midland characters when we remember that their lives might quite
literally depend upon it. And though nature is usually portrayed as a
beneficent, sustaining force in the journal, in a half-dozen notable
stories, it is malevolent.[20] These stories, among the grimmest and most
pessimistic the magazine ever published, appeared throughout *Midland*'s
history; the best example, Walter Muilenburg's starkly realistic "The
Prairie," was printed in the first volume. In a sense it established a minor
Midland genre.

"The Prairie" opens as a young Eastern couple, dissatisfied with their
lot, decide to go west to farm. When they reach the prairie in early
spring, it invites them forward with its "soft, wandering colors," and
they easily set up housekeeping. When summer comes they begin to feel
"helpless, in the midst of a power before which their strength was
nothing." There is no rain; their crops become parched. By late summer
the prairie seems to them vicious, ironic, even mocking. When they
think things are at their worst, a fire sweeps over the prairie killing the
wife. The next morning just after the husband buries her, it rains on the
completely-burned-out crops. The story ends with the husband walking
away from the ruins: "All about, the prairie stretched away — cold,
dreary, lifeless" (1.270).

It is such a story as this that John Riddell undoubtedly had in mind
in his 1929 *Vanity Fair* parody of the "gloomy midwestern story," which
ended "She broke her arm at the elbow, just to hear it snap."[21] We must
remember, though, that the gloomy midwestern story was rare in *Midland*.
The despair that characterizes "The Prairie" is true in only a handful
of the almost 400 stories the journal published. And, significantly,
most of these few are set in the early nineteenth century when the Midwest was first being settled. The vast majority of the journal's stories
have contemporary settings. In these, the life of the farmer is portrayed
as hard, but it is not depressing or impossible as it is in "The Prairie."
In *Midland* fiction, nature is much less frequently a source of suffering
and death than it is of beauty and contentment.

Stories of the "Great War"

ONCE the United States was drawn into World War I in 1917, older writers like Edith Wharton, Dorothy Canfield, and Willa Cather tended to think of it as a Great War, as "a necessary, perhaps even a vital, challenge to our devotion," Hoffman wrote. Younger writers like Ernest Hemingway, John Dos Passos, and Thomas Boyd tended to think of it as "a monstrous hoax, an unendurable outrage committed by the elders, who were brutal, insensitive, and stupid."[22] In many ways *Midland* fiction was closer to the more stable, family-oriented world the older writers portrayed, but its fiction about the war was completely in the tradition of the more disillusioned, cynical younger writers. Frederick himself thought the United States should not have entered the conflict; most writers whom *Midland* published would have agreed with him.

A story published by the journal in May, 1917—the month before American men began signing up for the draft—enunciated the most commonly recurring theme in the magazine's war fiction: the difference between war as soldiers experience it and as nonparticipants imagine it. The story, set in a French village, centers on a patriotic old woman with four sons, each named for a Duke of Savoy; "before they were old enough to understand the words she uttered, she commenced to tell them of these dead soldier rulers to whom they must do honor." The village postmistress, who serves as a foil for the old woman, has a different view about the honor due France:

> "Is it France who bears them? France who weeps? No. It is the mother who gets no word, until one day a bit of metal comes in a government envelope. And that is the end. Sing the Marseillaise if you will, you who have no sons. But for me it is a lie to say that I give my boy to his country. I would never give him. It is that I have no choice." (3.133)

The postmistress conspires with the village abbé to allow the patriotic old woman to think three medals she receives signify her sons' bravery, rather than their death. The abbé withholds a fourth medal he receives until after the woman herself dies. That medal is for her last son who could not face another winter in the trenches, became a deserter, was caught, and shot.

Once American troops entered the war, stories began to appear in the magazine fairly regularly about the experiences of American soldiers during the fighting. Almost nowhere in these stories is there any talk of honor, duty, or patriotism. Instead we see only extreme suffering and death. In two stories[23] soldiers agonizingly wait death in field hospitals; wounds are described with a naturalistic directness:

> In his left lung, there lies a great, torn fragment of shrapnel, and when he coughs, it turns and writhes within him, lacerating its way through muscle and tissue, and severing the vessels that obstruct its course. Then strains of crimson steal across his lips, and, presently, great basins brim with his own blood. . . . (6.183)

As in Hemingway's novels, there is a cynicism and mistrust of noble words. In one of William March's stories the journal published, a private is gassed and abandoned by his retreating company. As he lies in the mud he tries to remember a single "noble" thing he has seen or done since enlisting. But

> he could remember nothing except pain, filth, and servile degradation . . . "By God, they sold me out!" he thought . . . "The things they said were all lies!" . . . He lay trembling at his discovery, his eyes closed, his lips opening and shutting silently. Then an unbearable sense of disgust came over him. (7.146)

If there is significant similarity between the *Midland* and the major war fiction, there is also a significant difference. In *Exile's Return*, Malcolm Cowley wrote that many of the young writers who enlisted in the war in effect cut themselves off from their past, from their families, from the land of their childhoods: "Somewhere behind them was another country, a real country of barns, cornfields, hemlock woods and brooks tumbling across birch logs into pools where the big trout lay."[24] This other country of barns and hemlock woods figured scarcely at all in *A Farewell to Arms, The Enormous Room,* and other major fiction about the war, but it figured prominently in *Midland.*

Midland soldiers often think about "the prairies and the mountains and the sea — of the beauty and the gladness — that is *home*" (6.185). In several stories the focus is on the people at home awaiting the soldiers' return.[25] Perhaps the most interesting of these is about a "humane" father, a "silent man, partly deaf, who drove regularly to church on Sundays, seldom spoke, and for recreation improvised chords and modulations on the reed organ." To this man, whose son has been taken by the draft, the war is a wholly unwarranted disruption of his life: "Well, let them go, the thousands, if they wanted to be fools: but let them let *him* alone, him and his, his acres and his barns and his boy" (6.130). When he gets word that his son has died in camp of pneumonia he tears the flag out of his window and burns it. He wires the army that he does not want any soldiers escorting the casket. When the casket arrives he rips off the flag, tramples it, and throws it away. During the funeral he ploughs. Then he goes mad. If his reaction is extreme, it nonetheless reflects the notion that emerges in almost every *Midland* story about the Great War: that it was an unredeeming, inexcusable, inhuman affair.

Midland Social Realism

IN 1920 Frederick wrote Mencken that although Mencken's earlier comments about the trend toward political writing interested him, "the whole field of politics in America seems to me inconsequential.[26] Unlike Floyd Dell's *The Masses* or *The New State,* which Ansley edited in 1922, *Midland* never discussed specific political, social, or economic questions editorially. Throughout its existence, though, it published stories that dealt so explicitly with political, social, and economic issues that they approached the line which separates fiction from propaganda, art from tract. Walter Rideout has shown that the period was a quiescent time for the truly "radical" novel in America, but that there was much "exploration of the class structure of America and of class conflict . . . at the level of pragmatic observation."[27] It is this pragmatic observation of unjust social conditions that allows us to call about twenty-five *Midland* stories examples of social realism, fiction which aims not only to inform the reader of unjust conditions but to arouse him to action.

Almost all early examples are set in regions of the country other than the Middle West. In 1916 and 1917, for instance, there are stories by John Amid about California farming areas. The rather stock characters in one of these stories recall earlier figures by Frank Norris and look forward to later ones by John Steinbeck. A boss, "the big man — the financier — the thin-nosed, sharp-eyed, non-resident owner of the nurseries," has become sole owner of one of the biggest farms "since by a skillful manipulation of the machinery legally in his hands he has been able to force his early partner's widow from the business" (3.230). On the night of the story, six deputies with rifles hunt a person they regard as a "desperado — a terrible character who had broken into one of the stores on the outskirts of the business district." The desperado is actually a scared, hungry worker who has broken into a store to get food. After losing his job in the city he had been taken in by a crooked employment agency who " 'had it fixed with the boss out here, I guess; he fired me the second day.' "

Other stories deal with Tennessee mountain people who dig up nails from ash heaps for a living; an Italian coal miner who dies craving light in a dark, wet mine; and tenant farmers in the South who, after desperately writing their senator about their plight, receive from him a package of seed. [28]

The longest and one of the purest examples of social realism in the magazine, Will Burt's "Compensation," published in 1925, chronicles conditions in the copper mines of Butte, Montana. That this story is in the earlier muckraking tradition is underlined by an editor's note which states that the author "has furnished The *Midland* with a mass of newspaper clippings supporting the facts used in his story." The story is about a bright young boy whose father is forty-six years old, bedridden, and dying of consumption. The father warns his son to stay out of the mines at all costs:

> "Now I say it ain't *right.* Go out to the flat and read the tombstones. See how old are the miners of Butte when they die — forty, forty-three, forty-eight; seldom one above fifty. . . . When I was sixteen, Tom, I went into the mines — for a few months. And I stayed for twenty-five years. The same pressure that drove me in, kept me there." (11.68)

The plot is melodramatic. We see the boy about to board the train that will take him to a healthy outdoor job. The next scene jumps to a fire in the mines, which one character stupidly blames on "the I. W. W. and the pro-Germans." Hundreds of men die needlessly because the mine owners have failed to install doors in the concrete bulkheads. At the end of the story the boy's parents, who had assumed their son was safe in the country, learn that he never boarded the train, having decided at the last minute to work in the mines just long enough to pay for his mother's needed medical treatment. His corpse is barely identifiable.

Socially oriented *Midland* stories set in the rural Midwest tend to be much less melodramatic, the issues much less severe. *Midland* farmers work hard, but the plains have been broken and new machinery makes some of their tasks easier. They generally own their own land and enjoy a prosperity that eluded many of Hamlin Garland's earlier figures. Even after the 1929 depression, fiction in the journal rarely recorded *actual* hardship among the rural midwestern population. In one 1929 story a farmer, just as he is about to make the last payment on his mortgage, finds a placard on the bank's door saying its assets have been frozen.

We see the reaction of him and several other people, and the situation forebodes at least some economic hardship; it is significant that no hardship is actually portrayed.[29] Another farmer in a 1932 story listens to talk about "the worst depression the country ever had." Yet, ironically, it is the success of the economy rather than its failure that bothers him. When he suffers it is from the noise of a nearby gasoline "hoodle bug" train, the neglect of his milkman who has given up his pair of grays and whizzes by at forty miles per hour, and the nagging of his wife who wants to buy an "electric combination egg-beater and cake-mixer." [30]

If the midwestern farmer's life was almost always presented as reasonably prosperous in *Midland* fiction, the life of the midwestern urban worker often was not. In a 1917 story a waiter in an exclusive Michigan Avenue restaurant feels the sting of difference between himself and the patrons who wear diamonds, talk of country clubs, and condescendingly tip him. The waiter sees in the city "the rich man riding upon the poor man's back" (3.121). Urban workers in other predepression stories simply cannot find steady work. [31]

Understandably, the majority of the stories about urban suffering come after 1930 when the magazine itself (now in Chicago) was feeling the pinch of the depression. Characters who cannot find jobs are driven to desperate acts. In one story a decent man whose family is going hungry irrationally holds up a restaurant. In another an intellectual who speaks seven languages attempts to hang himself. A sixty-year-old man in still another story talks about dying in another way: "I couldn't likely get a job even if there was any work. They ought to chloroform us and put us out of the way. We'd be better off, I guess." [32]

These and other stories like them vividly remind us that, on the whole, the journal's fiction was not escapist. *Midland* fiction, at least in part, was related closely enough to contemporary social reality to reflect the proletarian strain that would dominate American literature in the 1930s.

Raymond Weeks and "Folk Humor"

THE journal's most frequently published prose writer was Raymond Weeks, an Iowa-born, Harvard-educated professor of romance languages who, during the *Midland* years, taught at Columbia University. Between 1918 and 1929 he published fifteen stories in the journal, almost all of which were humorous pieces that depended heavily upon the Missouri folk tradition he had become interested in earlier while teaching at the University of Missouri. Weeks's stories and a sprinkling of others like them in the journal might best be called examples of "folk humor." They seem related both to the late-nineteenth-century *Uncle Remus* stories and to the earlier American tales of boasting exaggeration exemplified by Davy Crockett's "autobiography." "The Hound-Tuner of Callaway," later the title story for one of Weeks's collections, is probably the best example of this strain of *Midland* writing.

Uncle Josh of Callaway County, Missouri, we are told, has developed a method for training the voice and the behavior of hound dogs through the use of a tuning fork. The story concerns his search, accompanied by his dogs, for his daughter Peggy, who has run off with a stranger of dubious background. After a three-month search he finds her, and together father and daughter return happily to Callaway County. The journey itself is reminiscent of the epic quest; regional details give it the comic flavor of the mock heroic:

> He took from a cache sufficient gold and silver to fill a money-belt, had well shod a young, powerful gray horse, named Robert in honor of General Lee, tossed into the saddlebags a change of linen and his best set of hound-forks, also his hunting horn, and rode softly away in the dead middle of a moonless night, accompanied by a hound escort of eight noble beasts. (12.335)

A number of things place the story squarely in the American folk tradition. Factual geographic details are embellished with highly fanciful local legends, and the story is told in the oral style. One narrator takes us through the first half of the story and then disappears except as a presence to whom the second narrator addresses asides — a device perfected in the nineteenth-century "frame" stories such as T. B. Thorpe's "The Big Bear of Arkansas" and Mark Twain's "The Celebrated Jumping Frog of Calaveras County." The effect here, as in the earlier stories, is to focus attention on the language of the second narrator, since the first narrator speaks standard English. In Weeks's story the first narrator describes the dogs accompanying Uncle Josh as "noble beasts"; the second narrator, an ex-slave, tells us a dog was "'runnin' along by the hoss as proud as Lucifah.'" The description of Peggy's beauty similarly becomes more powerful: "'She's thet puhty thet hit'd be a muhcy to the men to kill huh right now!'"

An oral style and an attempt at dialect characterize the "folk humor" stories. In many, an explicit distinction is made between the freshness of common speech and the "schoolmarm" English in books. One narrator is praised because he still speaks

the rich, beautiful dialect which crept up the rivers of Missouri in the first quarter of the nineteenth century, and was as much superior to the inane, school-marm English now to be heard as persimmon to paw-paw! (11.14)

Most of these stories have a robust, irreverent quality about them. Both the characters and the narrators often consume large quantities of liquor: "'Well! I'm prolonging this story beyond all reason! Pardon me, Willie, if I fill up my glass a third time — or is it a fourth?' " (11.7). And in a few of the stories we move to the amoral universe of the traditional American tall tale. One story, set in Vermont, is about an old man whose shrewish daughter loses her husband. She moves back in with her father and sanctimoniously empties his "cider" barrels one day while he is in town. After "drinking on it" with his cronies, he "kills her off" by stuffing his ears with cotton so he cannot hear her yell for medicine when one of her frequent heart spells comes on (7.103).

Editorially, *Midland* encouraged the recording of "riddles and folk remedies" (17.159) and spoke highly of efforts to preserve the authentic folk materials of America. Unlike *The Southwest Review* and some other regional magazines, however, the magazine never printed "pure" folk materials. Apparently its editors would have agreed with Hennig Cohen who, in "American Literature and American Folklore," argues that mere recordings of folk materials are lifeless and of minimum value since they can no longer grow through retelling:

> In a special sense, however, when folklore is made to function in a literary work it retains its vitality. In this sense folklore in American literature has had a long life and remains very much alive today. [33]

In this sense folklore, especially of the humorous variety, was much alive in *Midland*.

Midland Poetry

IT has frequently been observed that the poetry of regional little magazines is undistinguished. By and large, this is true for *Midland*. Frederick's tastes in poetry at the time were more conventional than his tastes in prose, and *Midland* never tried to specialize in poetry since Frederick was convinced that Chicago's *Poetry* was providing the best midwestern proving ground for young poets. Nevertheless, it is still puzzling to read some of the poetry the journal published during its beginning years. During the first year, for instance — the year in which two of Muilenburg's starkly realistic stories were published and in which *Spoon River Anthology* was singled out for a long, favorable review — the most prolific poet in the magazine was Mahlon Leonard Fisher. One contribution of his, published in the August 1915 issue, is entitled "Fancy":

He fills a dizzy cup for me: I dream
(As dreams the child, perchance, before 't is born)
Of lawns with all their grassiness unshorn,
And old aromas rising in a stream
So steadily inebrious they seem
To be the blended breath of all the flowers
Which fled from lockless insubstantial towers
The easy breezes ruined. I redeem
From sloth the shallop-shape that endless lay,
Long rotting, at unreal quays, and raise
A silk-and-silver ensign where it plays
With every zephyr; then forsake the bay —
The bay where late a flaming beacon shone —
And on a lonely sea set out alone!

(1.276)

Almost nothing about this poem suggests that it would have been appropriate for *Midland*. Quite the contrary. The nature of the experience — the person imaginatively escaping to sea in a small boat with the help of Fancy's dizzy cup — runs counter to the anti-romantic bias of the editorial policy. The words themselves — "perchance," "inebrious," "lockless insubstantial towers," "zephyr" — seem strange in a journal that favored realism in the use of language and speech. And the regular English sonnet form of the poem does not seem appropriate for a magazine that praised Carl Sandburg and Vachel Lindsay for capturing the spirit of the Middle West through their rougher verse forms. During the first year one ballad appeared, but its subject is distinctly non-midwestern: Mona Lisa. One of the only early poems to deal with what might be considered midwestern material, "An Indian Love Song," thoroughly romanticizes its subject:

I have seen him in the firelight when he stepped from
    out the forest
And he stood before my father with the flames upon his face.
Straight and tall and feather-footed and a quiver o'er
    his shoulder
And my heart leaped in the shadows for the fire of his embrace.

(1.223)

It is almost as if, during the first years, one group of men were shaping the editorial policies and choosing the fiction, and someone else who did not sympathize with them was selecting the verse.

Until the very end of *Midland,* there continued to appear a significant number of poems which we could classify as definitely nonregional, and the sonnet form remained popular throughout. Yet over the years a definite shift did take place. The poetry gradually, but never completely, became less traditional in its subject matter and less conventional in its form. The following lines by Jay Sigmund, published in 1924, recall some of the same values we noted in the journal's prose:

> Choosing a mate, he sought no comely form
> But looked for one to sweep his kitchen floor:
> He wanted one with hands to knead coarse bread —
> One with firm knees to grip a milk-pail's flanks
> And strength to carry water to his door.

(10.324)

Indeed, if Ruth Suckow's work best reflects the values of the magazine in the prose, Jay Sigmund's work probably best reflects those values in the verse. In one of Sigmund's 1925 poems, "Visitor," we have the reverse of the situation in Ruth Suckow's "A Rural Community." A person who "had kept deep-rooted in the clay" visits a friend who "had chosen market-place and street" and talks about "the things that happen where / The souls of men have kinship with the land." By the end of the evening the city dweller, like the journalist in Ruth Suckow's story, is unexpectedly moved:

> Then I who long had pitied peasant folk
>   And broken faith with field and pasture ground
> Felt dull and leaden-footed in my round
>   And strangely like a cart-beast with a yoke!

(11.343)

As the poetry gradually became more regional it tended to become both fresher and more interesting. The poetry of James Hearst, a regular contributor after 1925, at times recalls some of the specificity and freshness of Emily Dickinson's lines:

ROBIN IN THE STRAW

> A robin scratches right and left
> About the straw embroidered hem
> Of beds where flowers burst their shells
> But he is not in search of them.

He kicks out gayly with his legs,
He thrusts in wildly with his beak,
I wish I might encourage him
But he would fly if I should speak.

I stop my day to watch him work.
He pulls and winks his head about,
And spreads his wings and stamps his feet
When worm resists his coming out.

When I go plowing in the field
With hat and coat hung on a limb,
And sweat to hold my plow and team,
I wonder how I look to him?

(19.52)

Much of the verse the journal published was simply the description of a season, a piece of land, a bird. Only rarely did the poets attempt to show the relationship between the environment and man. One poet who did, Edwin Ford Piper, bears special mention in any discussion of *Midland* poetry. Piper, one of Frederick's early advisors and associate editor of the magazine throughout, was the magazine's most frequently published poet. His poems in volume three marked the first big break from the more traditional early verse. Some lines from a poem in volume twenty probably best suggest his ideas about poetry. He imagines Chaucer's thoughts before setting off with the Canterbury pilgrims:

Farewell to rhetoric and eloquence,
To the high style, the ink-encrusted word;
For measured tones of silken elegance
Let idiom in rough cadences be heard
While informality and humor plead
For speech that shall be cousin to the deed.

(20.36)

The deed Piper portrayed in most of his *Midland* poems was the settling of the prairies; during his Nebraska boyhood he had known many of the original settlers of the area. The language of his rough, blank verse is very much *not* high style:

The neighborhood
Is ready to mob me, and I've got to kill
Or be killed, and it's God damn tough on me!

(3.383)

Piper's titles suggest his concern with the commonplace in midwestern existence: "Barbed Wire," "The Windmill," "The Sod House," "The Well-Digger," "Grasshopper." Though his over-all tone is not elegiac, his verse reflects at least some sense of regret that the pioneer days have passed. In "Dry Bones," for instance, we see the buffalo who once "tossed/In great earth-shaking herds his shaggy mane" reduced to mountains of bones, "the price one dollar for a ton" (3.3). And in "The Last Antelope," we find that with the increased settling of the plains the antelope has become a caged, pathetic thing:

> Behind the board fence at the banker's house
> The slender, tawn-gray creature starves and thirsts
> In agony of fear. A dog may growl,
> It cowers; the cockcrow shakes it with alarm.

> (3.5)

Piper felt that, partly because of the strong sense of "community" midwesterners have, both the first settlers and their descendants have "A good world in the main" (3.366).

Probably the finest poet *Midland* ever published was Loren Eiseley. His work, published frequently during the journal's last several years, marks a high point toward which *Midland* verse as a whole was slowly moving. The concluding poem below suggest how different at least some of the later verse was from the rather artificial, optimistic, conventional verse of *Midland*'s beginning years.

COYOTE COUNTRY

> If you should go, soft-footed and alert,
> Down the long slope of shale
> Into a tumbled land of scarp and butte
> Beyond the pale
> Of the herding men, where water is under stone,
> You would be in coyote country. It is the place
> Where tumbleweed is blown
> Four ways at once, and your neighbors are not seen
> Except as loping shapes
> Or tangible dust.
> Once, if you're lucky, something may pause and lift
> One paw and two grey ears
> In a moment's trust
> That is gone like wind.

This is the road. Go down
Over the harsh way. If you dare, go down
Into the waste, where lonely and apart
The road runs north. Somewhere here is my heart
If anywhere. I spy
Nothing at all — and you in turn may try
The thistle and subtle stones,
Or you may go
Southward tonight — be certain you will not know
More of me than is found
In two poised ears
Or feet gone without sound.

(19.49)

Midland's Literature in Perspective

ABOUT half of the journal's poetry is of almost no interest to us to-day. It is traditional in form even for its time and undistinguished in content; some of it seems little different from the conventional, optimistic verse then being published in *The Saturday Evening Post,* a magazine the *Midland* editors singled out more than once as having a pernicious influence on American literature. The better half of the journal's poetry reflects more closely the regional bias of the magazine. It is a poetry of statement rather than of suggestion, and it lacks the richness or complexity of much other contemporary verse. Yet at its best, as in the work of Edwin Ford Piper or Loren Eiseley, it contains a freshness of vision that still makes it engaging reading.

Midland's prose is a good deal more consistent in quality. To be sure, there was little experimentation, and a pervasive factual realism tended to limit the things the authors could do — some of whom were publishing their first pieces. They could describe with facility and honesty the details of farming, the contents of a living room, and the speech mannerisms of people; but they were usually unable to plumb much beneath these more or less surface matters. A great, experienced writer — a Flaubert — might take the everyday life of a family in a rural community and show us something not only important but something compellingly important and exciting about the human condition. *Midland* authors did not.

On the other hand their work rarely seems contrived, particularly in the matter of plot, as does some of the contemporary fiction written for the large magazines by the major writers of the time. F. Scott Fitzgerald, for example, once wrote Edmund Wilson that he had "really worked hard as hell last winter writing eleven stories to pay off $17,000 in debts, but it was all trash and it nearly broke my heart as well as my iron constitution." [34] *Midland* authors were learning that the first requirement of a writer is that he write carefully and honestly, without an eye on salability. And *Midland* writers generally avoided the sentimentality that had characterized much local-color fiction.

If we conceive of American literature during the *Midland* years, from 1915 to 1933, as a pyramid, the journal's stories would occupy a stratum somewhere in the middle — below the work of Sherwood Anderson, Ernest Hemingway, and a few other major writers, but above most of the genteel, patterned stories in the large magazines. If *Midland* fiction lacked the brilliance of the work at the apex, it served as an antidote to the great mass of commercially-inspired, popular work at the base.

All things considered, *Midland* literature is a body of work for which any journal might proudly claim responsibility. Especially one which began modestly, existed without endowment for eighteen years, and was sustained largely through the efforts of one man.

NOTES

1   Austin M. Wright, *The American Short Story in the Twenties* (Chicago, 1961), p. 370.
2   George J. Becker, ed., *Documents of Modern Literary Realism* (Princeton, 1963), p. 29.
3   Wright, pp. 29-30.
4   The journalist has left his "family," but he is an adopted rather than a blood member. This distinction seems to have been an important one for *Midland* authors. In three other stories about adopted children, the only child that becomes fully a part of his new family is a child adopted by a bachelor who had once been in love with the child's mother and had been ready to marry her (see Abbott's "The Powerful Wobberjohn" [1.401]). In Van Horne's "The Curse," (3.162) a rich, crippled man attempts to adopt a child but is rebuffed by the authorities at the orphanage. And in Fisher's "Camilla," (19.70) a couple returns a child they have come to love after finding out the child's real mother was of questionable moral character.
5   See, for example, Reely's "Mothers' Day" (3.141); Suckow's "Uprooted" (7.83); Suckow's "The Resurrection" (7.217); Hartley's "The Late Joseph West" (10.260); Coonradt's "Effie" (14.7); Summer's "Home from Californy" (16.277); Derleth's "Geese Flying South" (20.37).
6   See Muilenburg's "The Ways of His Fathers" (8.81); Schnabel's "Bard Christjan" (18.124); Muilenburg, "Brothers of the Road" (2.266); Sundermeyer's "World-Gate" (13.287); Shelley's "Prodigal" (18.68).
7   Reely's "Mothers' Day" (3.141) and Coonradt's "Effie" (14.7), for instance, are about erring family members—a son who had spent six months in prison, and the wayward daughter of a prominent politician. In both stories there is some initial dissension, but the prodigal is taken in.
8   Shumway's "The Kiss" (19.60).

9   Wright, p. 91.

10 See Friedrich's "Emancipation" (14.106) and Roe's "Young Petroski" (20.22).

11 Wright, p. 56.

12 In Beloin's "Baby" (19.107), a nineteen-year-old proposes marriage to an older woman with whom he has just slept. She laughs at him. In Lull's "Just Before the Curtain" (18.108), a San Francisco painter who is "not the marrying kind" is sleeping with an impressionable girl. By the end of the story the painter emerges as a thoroughly insensitive egoist.

13 Wright, p. 151.

14 Frederick J. Hoffman, *The Twenties* (New York, 1965), p. 113.

15 Wright, p. 31.

16 See Hartwick's "Inquiry After Health" (15.117); Coates's "Stubborn Thistles" (17.26). For portraits of old people more typical of the journal see Rouse's "The Postage Stamp" (5.75); Crosby's "Space of Years" (9.25); Hartley's "The Late Joseph West" (10.260); Metcalfe's "Gentlefolk" (18.177).

17 Only 46 out of 384 *Midland* stories are set in a city, here defined as a community likely to have a population of more than 5,000; this determination was, of course, highly subjective. In about half of the 46 stories, the city is recognizably Chicago.

18 Hoffman, *The Twenties*, p. 119.

19 Brownell's "The Quest" (5.220).

20 See Muilenburg's "The Priaire" (1.260); Quigley's "But the Earth Abideth Forever" (2.6); Goodman's "Thomas" (8.145); Coates's "Glass" (16.17); Ward's "Drought" (18.197); Sullivan's "The Robin" (19.35). Muilenburg published a later novel also titled *The Prairie*.

21 John Riddell, "J. Riddell Memorial Award Best Short Stories," *Vanity Fair*, April 1929, p. 95.

22 Hoffman, *The Twenties*, p. 67 and p. 77.

23 See Imrie's "Remembrance" (6.182); Stout's "Plumes" (10.223).

24 Malcolm Cowley, *Exile's Return* (New York, 1951), p. 43.

25 See, for example, Muth's "The White Wake" (5.3); McIntyre's "A Man's Reach" (5.140); Stout's "Dust" (10.211); and Hunting's "The Soul That Sinneth" (6.128).

26 Letter from Frederick to Mencken, 3 November 1920; in New York Public Library.

27 Walter B. Rideout, *The Radical Novel in the United States, 1900-1954* (Cambridge, 1956), p. 115.

28 See Kroll's "Nails" (13.236); Hartwick's "Light" (13.104); Russell's "The Sandpile" (20.11).

29 Sigmund's "The Placard" (15.36).

30 Herrick's "Depression" (19.154).

31 See Barrett's "The Nettle" (9.157); Murtha's "Fragment" (12.240).

32 See Croghan's "Canvassers Neat Appearing" (17.117); Rice's "Monkey Business" (15.69). The quote is from p. 49 of Clarke's "Depression" (17.43).

33 Hennig Cohen, "American Literature and American Folklore," *Our Living Traditions* (New York, 1968), p. 247.

34 See Hoffman, *The Twenties*, p. 122.

Index of Contributors: 1915-1933

REFERENCES to stories and essays are followed by title of story or essay in parentheses. References not followed by parenthetical title indicate a poem, or a group of poems.

Abbott, Avery: 1.401 (The Powerful Wobberjohn); 2.345 (The Little Anna from Poland); 10.202
Abbott, Keene: 1.8 (Silent Battle); 3.15 (Bad Medicine)
Aber, Caroline E.: 10.387 (Morituri)
Adams, Simeon: 18.104
Albee, George: 19.130 (The Prince)
Alexander, Hartley Burr: 1.45 (The Pixie); 1.177; 1.397; 2.61; 2.181; 2.311; 3.80; 3.414; 4.170; 4.331; 7.329; 7.421; 8.216
Allen, C. S.: 2.218 (The State University and the "Great Society")
Allen, Harbor: 13.50 (Caged)
Allen, Sally Elliott: 14.115 (Nothing Left); 15.83
Alling, Kenneth Slade: 7.65; 7.116; 7.322
Ames, Lucile Perry: 14.161; 15.24
Amid, John: 2.313 (The Cup as Planned); 3.226 (The Freeze); 3.336 (A Professor); 4.282 (An Offer to Buy)
Anderson, Maxwell: 5.73
Appel, Benjamin: 18.105 (The Turners Become Wealthy); 18.180 (Rabbit); 19.57 (Brook Boundary); 19.93 (The Cup That Held Infinity)
Arbuckle, Mary: 7.177 (Wasted); 10.335 (Mirage)
Arnstein, Flora J.: 17.58; 17.154
Atkins, Elizabeth: 2.342; 4.281

Babb, Sanora: 20.29 (The Old One)
Babb, Stanley E.: 10.351
Bailey, L. H.: 4.103 (Can Agriculture Function in Literature?)
Baker, Karle Wilson: 7.446
Ballard, Adele: 3.130
Bard, William E.: 15.262
Barrett, Harold James: 9.157 (The Nettle)
Bates, Esther Willard: 4.272
Beadle, John A.: 18.94 (In the Shadow of the Windmill); 18.187 (Trace of Man); 20.32 (First Words)

Beardslee, Jean: 16.149

Becker, Charlotte: 5.19

Beems, Griffith: 19.95 (Brief Holiday)

Belitt, Ben: 16.314 (The Door Swings Wide); 18.114 (Not to Lethe);
19.53 (Case of Blasphemy)

Bellamann, H. H.: 6.41; 6.62; 6.153; 8.178

Beloin, Edmund: 19.107 ("Baby")

Benjamin, Paul Lyman: 4.1; 5.18

Bittner, Nelson Del: 18.119; 18.147

Bixler, Paul H.: 16.344 (Zigaboo)

Black, MacKnight: 10.322

Blanden, Charles G.: 2.327; 4.269; 8.340

Blankner, Fredericka: 16.290

Borst, Beatric West: 8.342

Borst, Richard Warner: 5.71; 5.139; 7.140; 7.415; 8.343; 10.250; 11.339;
13.229; 16.30; 16.187A; 17.70; 18.57

Bradley, Doris Lucile: 11.350; 15.220

Brady, Anna Mae: 18.117 (Travel is Broadening)

Bragdon, Clifford: 16.65 (Suffer the Little Children); 18.87 (Love's So
Many Things)

Bragin, Moe: 16.170; 17.60 (Cake); 19.50 (Flowers and Weeds)

Branch, E. Douglas: 11.237; 12.352 (Mr. Wainscot Awaits His Lady);
16.15, 18.58

Brant, Irving N.: 1.70; 2.103; 2.118; 7.82; 8.79; 9.37

Brigham, Johnson: 1.272 (Literature Local and General)

Boogher, Susan M.: 4.275

Brooks, Cleanth, Jr.: 15.220

Brownell, Agnes Mary: 15.254 (Sanctuary); 5.220 (The Quest); 6.138
(The Cure); 7.26 (Doc Greer's Practice)

Bruncken, Herbert: 4.69

Bryner, Edna Clare: 12.177 (Forest Dweller); 13.12 (The Ballad of
Hannah Silvis)

Bryson, Lyman: 2.113; 2.233; 3.198 (Under a Roof); 4.27 (A Man's
Word)

Burklund, C. E.: 16.167A; 17.41

Burnshaw, Stanley: 9.291; 12.355; 13.129

Burt, Will: 11.57 (Compensation)

Buss, Kate: 3.132 (Medals)

Byers, S. H. M.: 1.377

Bynner, Witter: 3.97; 4.273; 10.74; 11.336

Cain, Charles: 9.217 (Late October)

Calland, Annice: 11.170

Campbell, Eleanor Barnhart: 15.266 (Loafer); 16.297 (Restitution); 20.3 (Rich People)
Carroll, Dudley: 22.276 (Yellow Annie)
Carter, Russell: 10.246
Carver, George: 7.369; 8.95 (The Singer); 9.133 (The Scarlet One)
Cason, Clarence E.: 12.288 (Of My Uncle Harry)
Cassel, Miriam: 4.207; 6.88; 7.54; 10.334
Chandler, Josephine Craven: 8.346
Chapman, Edith: 7.425; 8.127 (Growing Pains); 18.196
Chapman, Frances Norville: 12.113 (Broken Rhythms)
Chapman, Kate Muller: 11.331
Chawner, Mary G.: 2.166 (Teacher Sylvia)
Cherryman, Myrtle Koon: 8.179
Childs, Marquis W.: 14.60 (A Journey); 14.186 (A Good Dinner); 18.2 (Renascence)
Chipp, Elinor: 3.415; 12.134
Clark, Dan Elbert: 2.33 (The Appeal of the Middle West to the Literary Historian)
Clarke, Cyril John: 17.43 (Depression); 19.9 (Cinemania)
Cline, Leonard Lanson: 8.277; 10.14; 10.199; 10.288; 12.49 (If There's Men There's Mermaids); 13.33 (Mekku)
Coates, Grace Stone: 10.413; 11.229; 12.159; 13.88 (Le Bonnet Rouge); 13.129; 13.179 (The Flyleaf in the Book of Disillusion); 13.190; 13.198; 13.226 (Crickets); 13.281 (Black Cherries); 13.323 (The Truth); 14.70 (The Nymphs and Pan); 14.138; 16.17 (Glass); 17.26 (Stubborn Thistles); 18.37
Coburn, Mrs.: 1.88 (Impressions and Comments on the Drama in America)
Coleman, Margaret P.: 17.70 (Dune's End); 18.32 (Before Breakfast); 18.168 (Afternoon in a House)
Collier, Tarleton: 5.130 (The Gracious Veil)
Cone, Marjorie: 12.27 ("Wie Eine Blume")
Connelly, Lebelva: 18.144 (Hoe-Help)
Converse, Blair: 10.161 (Black Furrows)
Cook, Harold Lewis: 11.172; 11.293; 11.349
Cooksley, S. Bert: 11.349; 13.145
Cooley, Julia: 2.367; 3.33; 4.253
Coombes, Evan: 18.183 (Kittens Have Fathers)
Coonradt, Paul: 14.7 (Effie); 15.163 (Down by the Tracks)
Cooper, Hoyt: 2.297; 5.44
Corbin, Alice: 11.323
Corey, Paul F.: 16.151 (Onlookers)

Costanzo, Rebekah Crouse: 16.293

Cover, Frederick: 16.149A

Cowdin, Jasper Barnett: 6.156

Crabbe, Bertha Helen: 9.207 (The Dog-Catcher)

Craft, Magdalene: 5.93 ("Blessed Are the Dead")

Crane, Frances: 11.263 (The Visit)

Cranmer, Catharine: 7.139; 7.312; 8.36; 8.333

Crawford, Nelson Antrim: 3.34 (The Golden Dawn Time); 5.164;
    7.419; 8.249; 9.65; 9.67 (The Fancies of the Practical Man); 16.290

Crew, Alice Hargrove: 11.169

Crew, Helen Coale: 6.95 (The Parting Genius)

Crocker, M. E.: 3.248

Croghan, Harold: 15.207 (Crazy About Her); 16.31 (A Pain in the Side);
    17.8 (A Good Boy); 17.117 (Canvassers Neat Appearing); 18.111
    (Jim); 20.1 (He Found Shelter)

Crookston, H. N.: 10.140 (Clay)

Crosby, Jane Snowden: 19.37 (The People Who Go to Museums)

Crosby, Katharine Kingsley: 2.105 (The Crowning)

Crosby, Marion: 9.25 (Space of Years)

Cunningham, Nora B.: 8.80; 9.206; 9.235; 10.325; 13.247; 13.275; 14.136;
    14.292; 16.187

Curtis, Christine Turner: 19.75 (Aquarelle)

Davies, Mary Carolyn: 3.129; 4.251

Davis, Charles F.: 2.362 (Nino Jesu)

Davis, Frederick: 12.147 (The Stranger)

Dawson, Mitchell: 11.346 (Any Young Man)

DeJong, David Cornel: 16.367; 17.59; 17.154; 18.136 (The Old Man)

Derleth, August W.: 19.5 (Old Ladies); 20.37 (Geese Flying South)

Deutsch, Babette: 4.180

Dixon, Jeannie Begg: 19.94; 19.138

Dolch, E. N., Jr.: 3.192

Dolliver, Frances Pearsons: 16.179 (The Old Man)

Drake, Sidney: 11.344; 13.69 (Goldenrod); 13.191; 13.322

Draper, Edythe Squier: 13.192 (As It Began to Dawn); 14.273 (The
    Fruit at Singapore); 16.129 (Fourteen)

Dresbach, Glenn Ward: 3.110; 3.193; 3.254; 4.45; 4.49; 5.216; 6.92;
    6.127; 6.178; 7.172; 7.257; 7.437; 8.180; 8.356; 10.191; 13.209; 13.250;
    14.37; 14.79; 14.240; 15.114; 15.176; 16.97; 16.168; 16.257; 17.25;
    18.107; 18.139

Dudley, Henry Walbridge: 12.1 (Query)

Dugan, Frances Dorwin: 7.297 (The Outsider)

Dumont, J. R.: 16.129A (You Must Forget)

Dunbar, Aldis: 3.320
Duncan, Thomas W.: 15.162; 16.147; 18.21 (Death of a Champion); 18.149

Edwards, Alice Mavor: 9.47 (The Old Holland School)
Eiseley, Loren C.: 16.159; 16.182A; 18.54; 19.34; 19.49; 19.85; 20.42
Eldridge, Paul: 6.200
Elpers, Richard: 14.211
Emory, William Closson: 14.136; 16.56 (Quartet); 16.123; 18.58 (Etching in Frost); 18.162
Engle, Paul: 16.258

Farrell, James T.: 18.3 (Mary O'Reilley)
Faust, Henri: 10.353
Feinberg, Elizabeth E.: 14.39 (Olivia Sets Forth); 14.215; 14.300
Feinstein, Martin: 4.137; 5.16
Ficke, Arthur Davison: 1.6; 2.197; 7.409
Field, Mildred Fowler: 11.190; 12.305; 14.6; 14.200 (Vessel of Life); 16.150; 16.357 (Mariner's Sarcophagus); 18.63
Fisher, A. E.: 17.13 (A Night at Sligo's); 18.8 (A Fine Woman); 19.70 (Camilla)
Fisher, Mahlon Leonard: 1.137; 1.196; 1.217; 1.276; 2.5; 2.93; 2.163; 2.165; 2.265; 3.51; 3.225; 4.44; 5.70; 5.209; 8.328
Flanagan, Dorothy Belle: 14.225 (Brave Guy)
Forsyth, Louise: 15.251 (Mr. Pemberton and Ladies)
Foster, K. K.: 7.113; 8.168
Fraiken, Wanda I.: 4.308 (The Harbor of Friends); 5.101 (Love Everlasting); 6.105 (The Rubber-Tired Buggy)
Frank, Florence Kiper: 2.280 (The Furlough); 3.196; 4.55 (The Child and the Little Sister); 5.168 (A Day)
Frederick, Esther: 2.41 (Uncle Al)
Frederick, John T.: 2.18 (Twelfth Night at Fisher's Crossing)
Friedrich, Irma: 14.106 (Emancipation)
Fuller, Ruth: 1.393 (Heilige Nacht)

Gallatin, Neal: 12.145
Gardner, Ella Waterbury: 2.200 (Ardena Prefers Sewing)
Garnett, Louise Ayers: 14.138; 18.35
Gates, Robert: 15.42; 15.250; 16.259; 17.23
Gates, V. Valerie: 13.92; 14.26; 14.105; 15.261
Gethman, Helen: 18.26 (The Misters Smith)
Gessler, Clifford Franklin: 6.60; 7.55; 7.171
Gibson, Katherine: 13.334 ("Art Was Cut Out for Me")

Giddings, A. F.: 18.170 (The Hunters); 18.171 (The Neat Little Feller)
Gidlow, Elsa: 14.73 (Quando)
Gilchrist, Marie Emilie: 6.137; 7.428; 10.328; 11.315; 15.155; 16.35
Gilmore, Robert A.: 1.197 (The Alchemy of the Lady)
Glaenzer, Richard Butler: 4.167; 5.88; 6.176
Glines, Ellen: 15.23; 15.116; 15.203
Gode, Marguerite: 14.195
Goldberg, Albert: 18.54 (There is Always Time)
Goodman, Henry: 8.145 (Thomas); 9.81 (One of Them)
Gordon, Don: 18.97; 19.1; 19.147
Gordon, Florence Lee: 4.126
Gray, Agnes Kendrick: 4.270
Greenwald, Tupper: 9.177 (Corputt); 11.197 (At Good Old Newton:
    Two Stories of College Life); 12.41 (Wheels); 12.203 (The Picnic)
Griffin, Myron: 18.24 (Senior Ball)

Hahn, Mannel: 18.78 (Progeny)
Hall, Carolyn: 6.177
Hall, Frances: 7.173
Hall, Hazel: 5.90; 11.141 (Vignettes in Prose); 12.11 (Favorable
    Impression); 12.70 (The Appointment); 12.128 (Home)
Halper, Albert: 15.177 (The Goose Dinner); 16.169A (The Race)
Halverson, Delbert M.: 6.28 (Leaves in the Wind)
Hanft, Frank: 18.48 (Chanty's Lion); 18.154 (The Widow's Pickerel)
Harris, Robert J.: 9.38; 10.65 (The Red Beard); 10.178 (The Two
    Walls); 14.302 (Brahms); 15.3 (Anna); 16.355; 18.30; 18.173; 18.194
    (The Bell); 19.103; 20.16
Harrison, Don: 5.174 (The Mixing)
Harrison, Shea: 10.188
Hartley, Roland English: 9.189 (The Battleground); 10.260 (The Late
    Joseph West); 13.161 (Destiny); 15.193 (Success); 16.99 (Once Upon
    a Time)
Hartsock, Ernest: 15.68
Hartwick, Harry: 13.104 (Light); 15.117 (Inquiry After Health); 15.225
    (Veni Sancti Spiritus); 16.37 (A Chicago Idyll)
Haste, Gwendolen: 5.210; 7.56; 7.412; 8.313; 8.334; 10.274; 13.9
Hayes, H. Gordon: 15.264
Hearst, James: 12.237; 12.354; 13.183; 13.228; 13.265; 13.317 (Old Joe);
    18.1; 18.86; 19.52
Heberling, Helen: 1.218 (Salt Fork River Sketches)
Heinrich, Carl: 18.129 (For a Bigger and Better War)
Heller, Helen West: 7.320
Helmle, Katherine G.: 18.31 (Cashier)

Henderson, Rose: 6.231
Henderson, Ruth Evelyn: 13.260; 14.194; 15.84; 16.113
Herrick, Marvin: 19.154 (Depression)
Hickenlooper, Jean: 2.326
Hill, Marvin Luter: 11.288
Hilton, Charles: 14.281
Himlinsky, Sara: 15.15; 15.107
Hoffman, Phoebe: 4.281
Holbrook, H. Weare: 3.128; 4.102; 4.336; 5.136 (The Penitent); 6.40
Holden, Raymond: 6.3
Holloway, Roberta: 12.173
Hopkins, Louise V. M.: 1.225 (Roads — Past, Present, and To Come)
Hovey, Alma Burnham: 9.1 (Where's Minnie?)
Hoyt, Helen: 3.288; 4.171; 5.100; 11.133
Huckfield, Leyland: 4.22; 6.57; 6.89; 7.22; 7.66; 7.127; 8.281; 9.237;
    10.425
Hudson, Hoyt: 12.286; 14.294; 15.41; 16.289; 18.93; 18.190; 19.122;
    20.17
Hunt, Robert: 16.98
Hunter, Grace: 7.386; 9.23; 9.42; 10.175; 13.224; 15.204; 16.372
Hunting, Ema Suckow: 6.47 (Dissipation); 6.128 (The Soul that
    Sinneth); 8.204 (True Love)
Huse, Harry Goodhue: 12.160 (The Old Trail); 12.225 (The Halo)
Hutchinson, Ruth: 18.140 (Eyes)
Hyde, V. D.: 4.295 (Good Tidings)

Imrie, Walter McLaren: 6.182 ("Remembrance")
Innis, Mary Quayle: 19.123 (Substitute)

Jackson, Leroy F.: 3.318; 5.200
Jacobs, Edith Roles: 16.171 (Near to Her Heart's Desire)
Jacques, Florence Page: 7.330; 8.349; 9.235; 10.238; 12.110; 12.321 (A
    Thorn); 13.212 (One Day); 16.185
Javitz, Alexander: 13.185 (Where the Sea Is Strange); 14.296 (Singing,
    I Shall Barter My Stars . . .)
Jenney, Florence G.: 6.25; 9.41; 10.132
Jennings, Leslie Nelson: 4.21; 4.145
Johnson, George C.: 7.75 (Mill Sounds)
Johnson, Josephine W.: 20.26 (Winter Orchard)
Johnson, W. H.: 19.46 (Bozo)
Johnston, William: 6.56; 6.201
Jones, Alicia: 7.1 (The First Sorrowful Mystery)

Jones, Howard Mumford: 1.281; 2.39; 3.185; 6.24; 6.157 (Drigsby's
    Universal Regulator)
Joor, Harriet: 5.260 ('Toinette Sketches); 6.189 ('Toinette Sketches)

Kang-hu, Kiang: 10.74
Kantor, MacKinlay: 10.400; 11.195; 12.356
Kelley, Luise: 12.127 (Clang)
Kemmerer, John: 15.31 (Along the River)
Kenyon, Bernice Lesbia: 7.415
Kerr, Harold: 19.131
King, Grace E.: 19.136 (No Victory)
Kline, Burton: 2.145 (The Unlifted Latch)
Knight, Reynolds: 2.299 (The Inspiration); 3.112 (Clay); 5.271 (Melody
    Jim)
Knister, Raymond: 8.1 (The One Thing); 8.254 (Mist-Green Oats);
    8.329; 9.176; 10.1 (The Loading); 10.242; 11.168
Kohn, Walter F.: 14.36
Kresensky, Raymond: 11.352; 12.274; 14.1; 15.44; 20.7
Kroll, Harry Harrison: 13.236 (Nails)
Kronenberger, Louis, Jr.: 9.187

Laedlein, Laura Landis: 8.325
Laing, A. K.: 12.329; 13.86
Laird, William: 14.94
Lamb, Adrian: 9.188
Lamb, Louise: 9.56 (My Canal)
Langebek, Dorothy May Wyon: 6.6; 6.64 ("Seven")
Larkin, Margaret: 10.385
Lauer, Edward H.: 1.154 (The German Drama of the Present Century)
Lechlitner, Ruth: 11.255; 11.287; 11.355; 12.174; 12.194; 12.201;
    12.320; 13.116; 14.209
Leonard, William Ellery: 1.33; 1.151; 1.330; 2.194; 7.416; 10.257
Levitt, Saul: 19.158 (Symphony After Midnight)
Lewis, Margaret E.: 20.7 (An Evening's Incident)
Lichtenstein, Vernon: 14.139 (A Morning in June)
Lincoln, Elliott C.: 7.426
Lindsey, Olive: 7.117 (Brief Possessions)
Little, Eleanor J.: 9.51 (Out of Fever)
Long, Haniel: 9.105; 11.33 (Notes for a New Mythology); 11.329;
    16.82; 17.100; 18.34; 19.78
Loudenback, Helen A.: 15.183 (The Worker)
Lull, Roderick: 18.108 (Just Before the Curtain)
Lull, Thelma Lucile: 12.64
Lytle, Leila Hill: 14.114

MacLeod, Geraldine Seelemire: 19.23
MacRae, Donald E.: 19.30 (Love)
McBlair, Robert: 8.27 ("One of the Beautiful Few")
McCallum, Mella Russell: 2.238 (The White Stars); 4.66
McCarthy, John Russell: 5.50
McCaslin, Davida: 7.67 (To Remove Mountains)
McClellan, Walter: 4.97; 5.270
McGill, Anna Blanche: 2.279; 2.359
McGinley, Phyllis: 20.21
McIntire, Ruth: 4.2 (How the War Came to Big Laurel)
McIntyre, Clara F.: 5.140 (A Man's Reach)
McLaurin, Kate L.: 2.329 ("The Sleep of the Spinning Top")
McLeod, LeRoy: 12.10
McPeak, Ival: 1.333 (Long-Short-and-a-Long); 5.20 (Knowing Dad);
    7.335 (A Prairie Symphony)
Malam, Charles: 15.108
Mallatt, Lola: 13.321; 14.212; 15.91; 15.272
Malm, G. N.: 2.94 (The Messiah Chorus of Lindsborg)
March, William: 16.1 (The Little Wife); 16.331 (Fifteen from Company
    K); 17.134 (To the Rear); 18.131 (A Snow Storm in the Alps);
    18.163 (Mist on the Meadow); 19.162 (The Arrogant Shoat); 20.10
    (The Eager Mechanic)
Marks, Jeannette: 4.181 (Old Lady Hudson)
Martin, Maude Williams: 18.200 (The Fable of the Gentle Reader and
    the Founders of a School)
Masters, Helen Geneva: 10.446 (Cynthia: A Silhouette)
Mathison, Minna: 4.307
Maxon, Harriet: 7.260 (Kindred)
Mazurova, Alexandra: 19.2 (The Hen)
Merrell, Lloyd Frank: 7.141; 7.420; 8.215; 8.246
Merryman, Mildred Plew: 15.16 (Old Lady); 16.175A (Vacation);
    18.47
Metcalfe, Mary E.: 18.177 (Gentlefolk)
Miller, Nellie Bourget: 6.199; 7.427
Miller, Richard: 20.39 (Man Alone)
Mixter, Florence Kilpatrick: 4.70; 4.100; 5.98; 6.59; 6.174; 7.249;
    8.338
Mohn, Ora R.: 8.177
Moore, Virginia: 19.125 (Mister Piper's Moment)
Morden, Phyllis B.: 16.30; 16.260
Moreland, John R.: 8.126
Morse, Stearns: 10.359 (The Last House)
Morton, David: 5.49

Mott, Frank Luther: 6.202 (The Man With the Good Face); 10.80
 (The Freight Whistles In); 19.82 (Literature with Roots)
Muilenburg, Walter J.: 1.260 (The Prairie); 1.362 (Heart of Youth);
 2.266 (Brothers of the Road); 4.129 (The Last Spring); 7.159 (Peace);
 8.81 (The Ways of His Fathers)
Murphy, Charles R.: 3.108
Murtha, Thomas: 12.240 (Fragment); 14.307 (The Little Jew Card-
 Player); 15.59 (Story from a Mill-Yard); 16.84 (Smart Work)
Muth, Edna Tucker: 5.3 (The White Wake); 5.269
Myers, Walter L.: 1.111 (Mates); 2.64 (In the Uplands); 4.80 (Clouds);
 8.41 (Summoned); 12.307 (Foolsfaces)

Neihardt, John G.: 1.101; 1.271
Nelson, Charles Brown: 11.193; 11.290; 13.112; 13.199; 15.14; 18.20
Nethercot, Arthur H.: 18.72 (The Door)
Neumann, G. J.: 14.68; 14.185; 15.1; 16.185A; 17.6
Neville, Marion: 19.85 (The White Glass Deer)
Newton, Ruth: 16.49 (The Wedding Gift)
Nicholl, Louise Townsend: 3.360; 4.271; 5.211; 6.26
Nielsen, Ellen: 18.160 (Niels' Father)
Nordahl, Edwilda: 7.424
Nutt, Howard: 19.157; 20.54

O'Brien, Edward J.: 2.104; 2.186; 4.334
O'Connor, Jack: 17.125 (Bucolic Wedding)
O'Grady, R.: 1.72 (A Gun); 6.7 (Brothers); 7.391 (A Man's Enemies)
Oliver, Wade: 8.78
Olson, John Helmer: 20.17 ("Come and See")
Olson, Ted: 13.85; 13.286; 14.151; 15.188; 16.313; 18.65 (Capone,
 The New American Myth); 19.29; 20.34
Osborne, F. M.: 17.102 (Vinegar Berries)

Parker, Lockie: 8.169 (Minnie)
Parrish, Emma Kenyon: 19.99 (The Doll that Went to Heaven)
Peck, Glenna Hughes: 4.268
Peterson, Edwin L.: 14.123
Philpot, Ada S.: 17.148 (Outing)
Phlegar, Thelma: 13.333
Pinifer, Alice: 5.138; 6.104
Piper, Edwin Ford: 3.1; 3.52; 3.65; 3.98; 3.289; 3.362; 3.388; 7.146;
 7.206; 7.388; 7.432; 8.59 (The Land of the Aiouwas); 9.145; 11.189;
 12.18; 13.65; 17.132; 18.121; 18.174; 20.36
Po Chu-Yi: 10.74
Pollard, Lancaster: 14.150; 18.62

Porter, Kenneth W.: 20.9
Pressley, Janet: 10.240
Price, Charles: 18.13
Prosper, Joan Dareth: 11.356; 14.44; 14.253 (On Being a Stenographer on Jackson Street); 14.282
Purdy, Nina: 16.261 (The Road)
Putnam, F. S.: (see Jacques, Florence Page)

Quigley, Edward G.: 2.6 ("But the Earth Abideth Forever")

Randall, Kenneth C.: 19.116 (A Small Matter)
Rauch, Basil: 15.135 (Evening of Nibs)
Raymund, Bernard: 3.191; 4.333; 5.257; 7.142; 7.322; 7.441; 8.352
Rayner, George T.: 14.81 (Life and Death on Ninety-fifth Street)
Reely, Mary Katharine: 3.141 (Mothers' Day); 3.322 (A Doctor Goes North); 7.173; 8.113 (Hands); 16.160 (A Pot of Bulbs)
Reese, Lizette Woodworth: 3.257; 4.128; 5.97
Reinecke, John E.: 11.345
Rice, Jennings: 15.69 (Monkey Business)
Richardson, Mabel Kingsley: 4.169; 5.96; 7.212; 7.436
Riley, Lewis A., II: 11.326 (Autumn Drifting)
Ristitch, Lazar: 18.84 (Hambone)
Rivola, Flora Shufelt: 4.52; 5.161
Roe, Sigfred A.: 16.362 (Janey); 19.104 (Rout); 20.22 (Young Petroski)
Rosenbaum, Benjamin: 7.292; 10.73; 10.402; 12.275
Rosenblatt, Benjamin: 3.258 (The Madonna); 5.212 (Stepping Westward)
Roth, Samuel: 5.172
Rouse, William Merriam: 2.370 (The Strings of Earth); 3.82 (The Strength of Simeon Niles); 4.148 (Old Man Wamsley's Ghost); 5.75 (The Postage Stamp)
Rummons, Constance: 4.332
Russell, Helen B.: 14.162 (Clean Dirt)
Russell, Mary Porter: 20.11 (The Sandpile)

Sabel, Marx G.: 7.325
Saltzman, K. Eleanor: 19.131 (Elder Brother)
Santmyer, Helen: 7.145; 7.444; 8.185 (The Old Lilac Tree)
Sarett, Lew: 7.410; 11.301
Schlesinger, Helen: 13.257
Schmitt, Gladys F.: 15.57
Schnabel, Dudley: 18.14 (Load); 18.124 (Bard Christjan); 19.39 (One Minute at Addisonville)

Scholten, Martin: 18.191 (Sanctuary)

Scribner, Frederick: 19.148 (Good Animal)

Seiffert, Marjorie Allen: 5.46; 5.91; 8.25; 12.77; 19.91

Sergel, Roger L.: 1.381 (The Philosopher in Fairyland); 2.125; 7.223 (Glare of Circumstance)

Shambaugh, Mrs. B. F.: 1.249 (Amana the Church and Christian Metz the Prophet)

Shaw, Dorothy Stott: 15.67

Shaw, Marlowe A.: 3.321; 4.11 (Father Hugh); 8.30 (A Landlord of No School); 9.124 (Logs); 10.113 (Jake); 10.416; 11.292

Shelley, Leila: 18.68 (Prodigal)

Sherry, Laura: 8.337

Showerman, Grant: 3.280 (Summertime); 3.307 (Old Neighbors)

Shuey, Mary Willis: 4.249

Shultz, Esther: 19.81 (Little Girl Growing)

Shultz, Victor: 18.44 (Goth and Visigoth)

Shumway, Arthur: 18.37 (Larry Wade); 19.60 (The Kiss)

Sigmund, Jay G.: 8.245; 10.324; 10.403 (Blinkers); 11.342; 12.195; 13.49; 13.113; 13.130 (Subpoena); 13.199; 14.196 (The Gaff Maker) 15.36 (The Placard); 15.86 (The Way Out); 16.146; 16.284 (The Runaway)

Simonton, Irma: 16.115 (The Play's the Thing)

Smith, Clark Ashton: 6.46

Smith, Edna Robotham: 16.329

Smith, Lewis Worthington: 1.44; 1.258; 2.86 (Beauty and Order, the Old Question); 2.293

Smith, Ruth Maurine: 4.293

Songer, Ernestine: 19.79 (Oh, That I had Gills Like a Fish!)

Starbuck, A.: 1.102 (An Amateur Interview)

Starrett, Vincent: 8.182; 19.266

Stearns, Harold Crawford: 4.215

Stengelsen, Albert: 17.83 (Neighbors)

Stephenson, Geneva: 15.248

Stevenson, Philip Edward: 11.237 (Smitty, Goggles & Co.); 11.248 (Cactus Flowers); 11.335 (Earth and Heaven); 12.81 (In the Country); 14.27 (June Bride)

Stewart, Irene: 13.93

Stoltz, Ruth M.: 14.131 (The Aristocrat)

Stone, Luella: 15.92

Stong, Philip Duffield: 7.370 (Hymeneal)

Stork, Charles Wharton: 4.72

Stout, George L.: 10.211 (Dust); 10.223 (Plumes)

Sturgeon, Josephine: 10.283 (The New Suit)
Suckow, Ruth: 4.216; 7.83 (Uprooted); 7.150 (Retired); 7.217 (The Resurrection); 8.217 (A Rural Community)
Sullivan, Richard: 19.35 (The Robin)
Summers, Floyd G.: 15.45; 16.277 (Home From Californy)
Sundermeyer, Clarence: 13.287 (World-Gate)
Sutherland, Marjorie: 2.260; 3.161; 5.51 (The School Teacher)
Swinney, Mary B.: 4.110 (A Conquerable Soul)
Sylvester, Harry A.: 19.92 (Locker Room)

Tallman, Robert: 19.80
ten Hoor, Frederick: 14.37; 14.57; 14.113; 14.183; 14.311; 15.189; 16.16; 16.112; 17.81; 18.193
Terrell, John Upton: 15.109 (The Break); 18.98 (Afternoon Off); 19.113 (And in the End)
Tharp, Doren: 16.148
Thayer, Harriet Maxon: 8.346; 12.110; 13.168; 18.57
Thomas, Jean: 19.24 (Poure Hippo)
Thompson, Jessie M.: 8.248
Thompson, Mary Wolfe: 9.70 (Old Diz); 10.428 (Turtle); 11.101 (Two Stories Told by Lucy); 12.257 (Zinnias)
Thornton, Romilly: 2.91
Tieje, A. Jerrold: 1.309 (Autumn on the Upper Mississippi)
Titus, Harold: 18.150 (The Frame House)
Tower, Roy A.: 10.379
Trimble, Chandler: 4.20; 4.106; 4.208; 5.48; 5.162; 6.94
Trombly, Albert Edmund: 4.77; 5.2; 7.422; 8.344; 10.153; 12.351; 16.27; 16.272
Trowbridge, W. D.: 19.143 (Bicycle for Bill)
Tull, Jewell Bothwell: 7.407
Turnbull, Belle: 11.289; 17.40

Uschold, Maud E.: 13.223; 14.184; 14.293; 16.48; 16.293

Van den Bark, Melvin: 10.291 (Two Women and Hog-Back Ridge)
Van Dine, Warren L.: 10.44 (The Poet)
Van Doren, Mark: 10.330
Van Horne, Margaret Varney: 3.162 (The Curse)
Van Wyck, Eleanor: (see Coleman, Margaret P.)

W., E.: 4.99
Wade, Harmon C.: 9.38
Wadsworth, Euleta: 4.172 (The Message)
Wallace, John H.: 3.224

Ward, Father Leo L.: 14.207 (Black-Purple in the Corn); 14.283
(Possession); 15.133 (After Cornhusking); 15.145 (Balaam in
Burrville); 15.215 (Rust in the Wheat); 15.218; 16.118 (The Rain);
16.151A (The Threshing Ring); 18.197 (Drought); 19.67 (Cutting
Dock); 19.141 (Newfangled Machinery); 20.42 (Tobe Snow)
Ward, Leo R.: 20.35 (Ike and Em)
Ward, Louis L.: 13.1 (Master and Servant)
Watson, Jean: 9.43 (Good People)
Wattles, Willard: 1.223; 1.361; 2.55; 2.183; 3.78; 3.353; 4.73; 4.209
Weaver, James B.: 1.22 (The Authors' Homecoming of 1914)
Weaver, Ray Bennett: 2.234; 2.361; 4.98; 4.252; 7.132 (The Web on
the Altar); 7.313; 7.411; 10.321; 11.89; 12.121; 13.97; 13.233; 14.25;
14.137; 14.210; 14.301; 15.43; 15.82; 18.43
Weber, Lee Andrew: 11.165; 11.351; 13.248; 16.187
Weeks, Raymond: 4.217 (How I Burned for Heloise); 4.229
(Sawbuttee); 4.233 (Where is Tennessee?); 4.277 (The Canadian
Forest); 7.253 (The Canaries); 7.256 (Tricolor); 7.319; 9.112
(Arkansas); 10.27 (The Bucking Palfrey); 11.1 (The Fat Women of
Boone); 11.12 (The Snakes of Boone); 11.19 (On the Road to the Big
Blue); 11.23 (Two Gentlemen from Indiany); 11.27 (Thou Canst Not
Say I Did It); 12.330 (The Hound-Tuner of Callaway); 14.259 (The
Two Hands)
Welch, Marie de L.: 13.28
Weston, Mildred: 10.332
Whitcomb, Selden L.: 1.36 (Spring — A Mental Ramble); 1.186
(Summer Days by Prairie Waters); 1.321 (Dominant Themes of
Autumn); 1.418 (The Spirit of Winter)
White, Nelia Gardner: 13.266 (Toby Hatch); 14.241 (The Wish); 15.97
(Aunt Maria)
Widdemer, Margaret: 4.10; 4.108
Wilkinson, Marguerite: 2.344
Williams, Oscar: 7.58; 7.114; 7.430; 8.215
Wilson, Henry L.: 14.125 (The Muse Plays Chess)
Wilson, Lida Patrick: 10.280 (For Rent — An Old-Fashioned House)
Wintrowe, Norine: 7.334
Wood, Clement: 4.78; 4.139
Wood, Gracia Pope: 8.325
Woodall, Allen E.: 15.130
Wright, J. Ernest: 10.154; 10.377
Wyer, Malcolm G.: 1.53 (The Drama League of America)
Wylie, Robert Bradford: 2.114 (Trees and the Homestead)

Zaturensky, Marya: 11.340

Index to *Midland* Book Reviews

INDEXED below are authors of works of any nature (e.g., fiction, criticism, history) reviewed in *Midland.* Biographies and critical works on a single person are also indexed under the subject of the work. Works by joint or multiple authors are indexed under each author; works translated are indexed under the original author and the translator. Editors of anthologies are not listed.

In *Midland,* reviews appeared either in the regular book review sections ("The Midland Library" and "I've Been Reading"), which generally contained only short reviews, or in individual articles, which were usually several pages in length. Citations with asterisks are to the separate, longer reviews.

In volume 16, pp. 129-92 are mistakenly repeated. Citations here to the second series of these numbers are designated with an "A."

Abbott, Keene: 2.134*
Adams, Edward C. L.: 13.279
Adams, James Truslow: 16.124
Aiken, Conrad: 11.254; 12.112; 15.141; 16.190
Alarcon, Don Pedro de: 14.318
Alexander, Hartley B.: 2.119; 8.326*; 11.338
Alger, Horatio, Jr.: 14.219
Allen, Hervey: 11.308; 12.254; 16.63
Anderson, Emily: 10.382
Anderson, Margaret: 16.190A
Anderson, Sherwood: 7.110*; 8.297*; 10.156*; 11.54; 12.358; 13.157; 13.258*; 14.54; 15.141
Angoff, Charles: 18.175
Applegate, Frank G.: 16.191A
Arnold, John: 15.54
Atherton, Sarah: 16.188A
Aurner, Clarence R.: 1.28
Auslander, Joseph: 12.363
Austin, Walter: 11.310
Austin, William: 11.310

Bacon, Leonard: 11.182
Bagby, George William: 15.55
Bailey, John: 13.30
Bailey, L. H.: 1.318; 2.58
Barry, Charles: 15.54
Beck, Henry Charlton: 18.176
Becker, May Lamberton: 10.422
Beebe, William: 12.39; 14.104
Beecher, Henry Ward: 14.101
Beer, Thomas: 10.159; 12.361
Belloc, Hilaire: 16.62
Bennett, Charles A.: 10.205
Bercovici, Konrad: 11.56
Best, Mary Agnes: 13.280
Bethea, Jack: 14.267
Bianchi, Martha Dickinson: 10.383
Bierce, Ambrose: 11.184
Bickle, Lucy Leffingwell Cable: 15.139
Bishop, John Peale: 18.63
Blankenship, Russell: 18.175
Blankner, Fredericka: 20.28
Bleyer, Willard Grosvenor: 13.158
Bodenheim, Maxwell: 13.201
Bogan, Louise: 10.318; 16.127
Bojer, Johan: 12.255
Boker, George Henry: 14.100
Bond, F. Fraser: 18.91
Bontemps, Arna: 19.28
Bose, Sudhindra: 12.300
Bourdin, Henri L.: 12.75
Bowman, John G.: 13.152
Boyd, Ernest: 12.140
Boyd, James: 11.295*; 13.251
Bradford, Roark: 15.52; 15.157*; 19.28
Bradley, Edward Sculley: 14.100
Braley, Berton: 1.391
Branch, Anna Hempstead: 16.64
Branch, E. Douglas: 13.200; 15.95; 16.373
Brigham, Johnson: 14.96
Brooks, Van Wyck: 11.187; 13.203
Broun, Heywood: 13.206
Brown, Alice: 1.96

Brown, Henry Collins: 13.120
Brown, Rollo Walter: 11.196; 15.139; 18.202; 20.55
Browne, Francis Fisher: 1.60; 1.319
Brownell, Agnes Mary: 7.143*
Brownell, W. C.: 11.162
Bryner, Edna: 13.151
Bryson, Lyman: 3.28
Bullard, Lauriston: 1.319
Bunyan, Paul: 11.294; 19.55
Burdette, Robert J.: 1.29
Burke, Kenneth: 11.87
Burnham, David: 17.159
Byers, Major S. H. M.: 1.27; 1.244; 2.121
Bynner, Witter: 10.111
Byrne, Donn: 11.99; 11.183

Cabell, James Branch: 11.162; 11.179; 12.200
Cable, George W.: 15.139
Calverton, V. F.: 19.166
Canfield, Dorothy: 2.261; 10.110
Cannon, Cornelia James: 14.267
Carroll, Gladys Hasty: 20.55
Carson, Kit: 1.61; 14.218
Cather, Willa: 2.123; 12.139; 19.139
Catlin, George: 10.160
Cawein, Madison: 1.60
Cestre, Charles: 18.35
Chamberlain, George Agnew: 10.384
Chapman, Maristan: 14.268
Charnwood, Lord: 1.319
Chase, Cleveland B.: 14.54
Chase, Stuart: 16.124
Chesnutt, Charles W.: 15.157*
Chittick, V. L. O.: 11.163
Christensen, Thomas P.: 14.217
Christie, Miss: 16.62
Chubb, Edwin Watts: 1.278
Clark, Badger: 11.254
Clark, Barrett H.: 13.205
Clark, Emily: 18.175
Cline, Leonard: 12.74; 12.302; 13.276
Coates, Grace Stone: 17.158; 19.56; 20.28
Collins, Caspar: 14.218

Comstock, Anthony: 13.206
Connor, Daniel J.: 11.183
Conrad, Joseph: 14.153
Cook, George Cram: 14.100
Coppard, A. E.: 11.307
Corbett, James J.: 11.179
Crane, Stephen: 10.159
Crawford, Nelson A.: 10.417*; 14.158; 17.157
Crevecoeur, St. John de: 12.75
Croce, Benedetto: 10.382
Cullen, Countee: 12.303; 13.121*; 14.98; 16.61; 19.111
Cummings, E. E.: 8.309*; 12.360

D., H.: 11.88; 12.198
Darrow, Clarence: 19.55
Davidson, Donald: 10.383; 14.53
Davis, Richard Harding: 14.102
Davis, Robert H.: 18.91
Day, Richard E.: 16.295
de la Mare, Walter: 11.129
De Mille, George E.: 18.148
Deacon, William Arthur: 10.63
Deledda, Grazia: 14.156
Dell, Floyd: 7.110*; 11.225; 13.94
Dickinson, Emily: 10.383
Dickinson, Thomas H.: 19.167
Dillon, George: 14.53
Director, Aaron: 19.168
Dobie, Charles Caldwell: 14.102
Dodge, Daniel Kilham: 11.87
Dodge, Grenville M.: 1.97
Donovan, Josephine: 16.294
Dos Passos, John: 8.19*; 10.109
Doster, W. E.: 1.319
Douglas, Paul H.: 19.168
Dreiser, Theodore: 10.422; 12.38; 12.281*; 14.318; 18.64
Dresbach, Glenn Ward: 8.326*; 13.119; 15.95; 16.126; 18.203
Drewry, John E.: 11.100
DuBois, W. E. B.: 14.220
Dudley, Louise: 14.317
Duncan, Isadora: 14.219
Duncan, Mr.: 14.54
Duncan, Thomas W.: 16.190
Dyer, Walter A.: 1.319

Eastman, Max: 18.35
Eaton, G. D.: 11.178
Edmonds, Franklin S.: 1.244
Ehrlich, Leonard: 20.27
"Elizabeth": 13.160
Ellwood, Charles A.: 1.172
Emerson, Ralph W.: 13.203
Emory, William Closson: 16.127
Ervine, St. John G.: 15.50
Evans, Abbie Huston: 14.316
Everett, Edward: 11.311

Fagin, N. Bryllion: 10.159; 12.254; 14.54
Faris, John T.: 10.319
Faulkner, Harold Underwood: 18.175
Fauset, Jessie Redmon: 15.157*
Ficke, Arthur Davison: 1.245; 1.391; 11.53
Finger, Charles J.: 10.203*; 11.176*; 13.277; 15.95; 15.279
Finley, Ruth E.: 19.112
Fish, Carl Russell: 14.217
Fisher, Mahlon Leon: 3.28
Fisher, Vardis: 15.94; 18.120
Flanner, Hildegarde: 16.63
Flecker, James Elroy: 12.359
Fletcher, J. S.: 15.54
Flitch, J. E. Crawford: 12.40
Foerster, Norman: 16.63
Foley, James W.: 1.60
Ford, Corey: 17.78
Ford, Ford Madox: 12.253; 14.153; 14.154
Foster, Thomas: 10.422
Franklin, Benjamin: 13.63
Frederick, John T.: 11.227
Freeman, John: 12.362
Frost, Frances: 10.28
Frost, Robert: 10.158; 14.55; 15.53
Frothingham, Paul Revere: 11.311
Furman, Lucy: 14.97
Fyfe, Hamilton: 18.91

Gabriel, Ralph H.: 12.75
Gale, Zona: 14.54
Gallagher, Marie: 11.100
Galsworthy, John: 12.328

Garland, Hamlin: 13.276; 15.48; 17.77
Gibran, Kahlil: 15.54
Gilbert, William: 15.55
Gilbreath, Olive: 12.199
Gilchrist, Marie Emilie: 12.252; 19.139
Glaeser, Ernst: 15.276
Glasgow, Ellen: 11.306; 13.95
Glaspell, Susan: 14.100; 15.49
Goethe: 10.382
Gohdes, Clarence L. F.: 19.112
Goldberg, Isaac: 12.140; 15.55
Goldring, Douglas: 13.29
Gorgione, Louis: 14.315
Gould, Bruce: 15.223
Graham, Cunninghame: 16.189A
Graham, Walter: 13.153
Grant, Ulysses S.: 1.244
Greeley, Horace: 14.101
Green, C. R.: 1.96
Green, Paul: 12.256; 13.204
Grinnell, George Bird: 1.318
Grove, Frederick Philip: 14.315

Hafiz: 15.53
Haight, Gordon: 17.77
Hale, Sarah Josepha: 19.112
Haliburton, Thomas Chandler: 11.163
Hall, Hazel: 15.95
Hall, James Norman: 13.205; 14.223
Hall-Quest, Alfred Lawrence: 15.223
Halper, Albert: 20.55
Hamilton, Clayton: 10.320; 11.164
Hansen, Harry: 10.110
Hare, Amory: 13.253
Harlow, Alvin F.: 18.175
Hartley, Olga: 14.269
Hartley, Roland English: 14.318
Harshaw, Ruth: 18.203
Haste, Gwendolen: 18.203
Hatcher, Harlan: 18.64
Hawthorne, Nathaniel: 14.100
Hayes, Edward C.: 1.318
Hazard, Lucy Lockwood: 13.154

Hazen, Alice: 1.172
Hazen, Charles Downer: 13.151
Hearn, Lafcadio: 10.420; 11.129
Hearst, W. R.: 14.219
Heinrich, Carl: 16.188A
Hellman, George S.: 12.198
Henry, O.: 18.91
Hemingway, Ernest: 12.138; 13.184; 15.277
Henderson, Alice Corbin: 14.316
Henderson, Charles Richmond: 1.277
Hergesheimer, Joseph: 14.318
Herrick, Robert: 12.361
Heyward, DuBose: 10.423; 13.184
Hibben, Paxton: 14.101
Holloway, Emory: 13.153
Holmes, Fred L.: 1.318
Horn, Alfred Aloysius: 13.261*
Hough, Emerson: 2.295
Hough, Walter: 1.62
How, Louis: 11.338
Howe, E. W.: 14.223; 15.140
Howells, William Dean: 2.92
Huch, Ricarda: 16.62
Huckfield, Leland: 9.261*
Hughes, Langston: 12.303; 13.121*
Hume, Cyril: 13.118
Hurst, Fannie: 14.156; 15.140
Husband, Joseph: 2.120

Irving, Washington: 12.198

Jacobson, Jens Peter: 11.227
James, Henry: 11.187
Jeffers, Robinson: 16.190; 18.96*
Jesus: 15.140
Jewett, Sarah Orne: 11.185
Johns, Orrick: 12.299
Johnson, Evelyn: 15.54
Johnson, James Weldon: 14.98; 14.99; 19.28
Johnson, Rossiter: 1.319
Johnson, Sir William: 16.295
Jones, Eliot: 1.135

Jones, Charles Reed: 15.142
Jones, Howard Mumford: 2.59; 14.217
Jones, Laurence C.: 10.206
Jones, Nard: 16.125
Joor, Harriet: 12.224

Kantor, MacKinlay: 14.271; 19.55
Kearton, Cherry: 17.156
Kellock, Harold: 14.218
Keyser, Cassius J.: 10.420
King, General Charles: 1.244
King, Joseph Leonard: 15.55
Knibbs, Henry Herbert: 1.26; 1.98; 2.263
Knister, Raymond: 15.278
Komroff, Manuel: 12.199; 14.97
Krapp, George Philip: 11.129
Kroll, Harry Harrison: 15.48; 18.202
Krutch, Joseph Wood: 12.300

Laing, A. K.: 13.280
Laing, Alexander: 15.96
Lane, Rose Wilder: 11.308
Lardner, Ring: 13.252; 15.141
Larsen, Hanna Astrup: 11.227
Lattimore, R. A.: 13.280
Lawson, John Howard: 11.185
Lawson, W. P.: 11.338
Leech, Margaret: 13.206
Leonard, William Ellery: 10.309*; 12.141
Lewis, Mrs. Ethelreda: 15.49
Lewis, Janet: 20.27
Lewis, Sinclair: 7.110*; 11.180; 17.1*
Lewisohn, Ludwig: 10.109; 15.54; 19.166
Leyel, Mrs. C. F.: 14.269
Lidin, Vladimir: 19.56
Lincoln, Abraham: 1.60; 1.319; 10.255; 11.87
Lincoln, Elliott C.: 10.421
Lindsay, Vachel: 1.97; 1.164*; 1.170*; 2.29; 3.356*; 12.143; 15.221;
    16.188
Lippmann, Walter: 14.101
Loggins, Vernon: 19.111
Löhrke, Eugene: 15.277
London, Jack: 11.308

Long, Haniel: 13.119
Long, Lilly A.: 1.27
Longstreth, T. Morris: 10.420
Lowell, Amy: 12.39; 14.221
Lovett, Robert Morse: 11.313
Ludwig, Emil: 15.54
Lynch, Denis T.: 14.101

Macleish, Archibald: 19.139
MacLeod, LeRoy: 19.139
Manhood, H. A.: 15.51
Mann, Thomas: 11.225; 12.197; 14.318
Manzoni, Alessandro: 11.183
March, William: 20.28
Markum, Leo: 16.295
Marnas, Mélanie: 15.140
Masters, Edgar Lee: 1.238*; 11.164; 12.224; 15.221
Maurice, Arthur B.: 18.91
Mayer, Brantz: 15.52
Mayes, Herbert R.: 14.219
McCarter, Margaret Hill: 2.92
McCaslin, Davida: 14.317
McClintock, Marshall: 17.160
McElroy, Robert McNutt: 1.27
McFee, William: 10.208
McKay, Claude: 13.121*; 14.220; 15.157*
Meigs, Cornelia L.: 2.120
Melville, Herman: 12.362
Mencken, H. L.: 12.140
Mervin, Samuel: 1.177
Millay, Edna St. Vincent: 10.207; 14.103
Millay, Kathleen: 15.142
Millen, Gilmore: 16.294
Miller, Charles R.: 18.91
Miller, Joaquin: 16.373
Mills, Enos A.: 1.96; 1.278
Milne, A. A.: 11.130
Milton, John: 1.26
Mixter, Florence Kilpatrick: 8.326*
Monroe, Harriet: 12.358
Montague, Margaret Prescott: 15.51
Moody, William Vaughn: 18.63
Moore, Julia A.: 14.221

Morand, M. Paul: 15.157*
Morley, Christopher: 13.278
Morris, Lloyd: 14.100
Morris, William: 12.139
Mott, Frank Luther: 16.124
Mott, Lewis Freeman: 11.186
Muilenburg, Walter J.: 11.302*
Mukerji, Dhan Gopal: 11.129
Muldavin, Albert: 18.176
Mullins, Helene: 11.100
Munson, Gorham B.: 14.55
Murasaki, Lady: 12.142
Murphy, Dennis: 19.56
Murphy, Thomas D.: 1.96; 10.456

Nathan, Robert: 11.225; 13.253; 14.53; 15.93; 17.160
Nearing, Scott: 1.277
Neihardt, John G.: 2.25*; 3.30; 8.315*; 11.309; 12.280; 13.64; 13.156;
    15.55
Nevins, Allan: 14.217
Newman, Frances: 11.162; 13.146*
Nicholson, Meredith: 2.295
Nixon, H. K.: 15.222
Norris, Charles G.: 12.363
Northcliffe: 18.91
Nye, Bill: 13.206
Nye, Frank Wilson: 13.206

O'Brien, Edward J.: 16.124
O'Donnell, Charles L.: 16.128
Odum, Howard W.: 14.220; 16.60; 16.375
Olivier, Edith: 13.279
O'Neil, George: 13.201
O'Neill, Eugene: 13.205
Oppenheim, E. Phillips: 16.62
Orrick, Johns: 12.299
O'Shaughnessy, Edith: 11.140
O'Sheel, Shaemas: 14.221

Paine, Thomas: 13.280
Palmer, Bessie Pryor: 13.204
Palmer, Gretta: 15.54
Parker, William Belmont: 1.138*
Parrington, Vernon Louis: 18.35

Paterson, Isabel: 16.187A
Patrick, George T. W.: 2.196; 11.178; 15.222
Pattee, Fred Lewis: 18.35
Perkins, Charles Elliott: 14.159
Peterkin, Julia: 11.99; 13.201; 15.92
Pettibone, Anita: 11.228
Pinski, David: 14.270
Piper, Edwin Ford: 10.100*; 13.158
Poe, Edgar Allen: 12.300
Pound, Arthur: 16.295
Powell, Lyman P.: 11.188
Power, Caroline Marguerite: 14.318
Preston, Keith: 12.143
Prichard, Katharine Susannah: 13.231
Putnam, Emily James: 13.158

Quick, Edward: 13.206
Quick, Herbert: 2.120; 11.164; 11.286; 12.138; 13.206

Rabb, Kate Milner: 11.88
Rascoe, Burton: 12.38
Read, Opie: 18.176
Redfield, Arthur Patrick: 14.158
Redman, Ben Ray: 13.202
Reece, Ernest: 1.277
Reed, Earl H.: 2.164
Remarque, Erich Maria: 15.276
Richardson, Lyon N.: 19.112
Ridge, Lola: 16.189
Rinehart, Mrs.: 16.63
Roberts, Elizabeth Madox: 14.51; 15.93; 17.159; 18.202
Robertson, William J.: 14.99
Robinson, Edwin Arlington: 11.184; 13.202; 13.252; 18.35
Roche, Mazo de la: 14.52
Rolvaag, O. E.: 15.93
Rosenbaum, Benjamin: 10.384; 17.79
Rusk, Ralph Leslie: 11.314
Russell, Bertrand: 10.319
Russell, Phillips: 13.63

Sabin, Edwin L.: 1.61
Sachs, Emanie N.: 10.382; 15.138
Sainte-Beuve: 11.186
Saki: 15.223; 17.76

Salten, Felix: 14.270
Sandburg, Carl: 2.189*; 13.207
Santayana, George: 18.148
Sarett, Lew: 12.36; 18.203
Sayers, Dorothy L.: 16.62
Schlesinger, Arthur Meier: 11.311
Schneider, Isidor: 14.221
Schnitzler, Arthur: 10.111; 13.117
Schreiner, Olive: 13.254
Scott, Evelyn: 10.61
Scott, Mansfield: 15.142
Seiffert, Marjorie Allen: 13.255; 16.127
Seitz, Don C.: 12.328; 14.101
Sergel, Roger: 10.57*; 10.64
Shaw, Marlow A.: 12.300
Sheehan, Murray: 13.252
Shively, George: 11.187; 13.153
Sigmund, Jay: 10.251*; 12.111; 13.143*; 13.231; 17.79; 18.63
Sigourney, Lydia H.: 8.77
Sill, Edward Roland: 1.138*
Simpson, William Haskell: 15.142
Singmaster, Elsie: 11.182
Skinner, Alanson: 1.62
Slosson, Preston William: 18.175
Smith, Arthur D. Howden: 13.93
Smith, C. Alphonso: 13.277
Smith, Elizabeth Oakes: 13.278
Smith, Lewis Worthington: 2.122
Smith, Logan Pearsall: 12.142
Smith, Seba: 13.278
Sparling, A. H. Halliday: 12.139
Speer, Faye Nixon: 1.60
Spring, Agnes Wright: 14.218
Stallings, Laurence: 11.181
Steele, Wilbur Daniel: 16.295
Steiner, Edward A.: 1.98; 2.31; 2.121; 3.29
Sterling, George: 13.31
Stevens, James: 11.294; 19.55
Stevenson, O. J.: 2.124
Stevenson, Philip: 15.191; 17.157
Stevenson, Robert Louis: 10.320
Stewart, Donald Ogden: 11.307

Stong, Phil: 19.139
Strahorn, Carrie Adell: 2.92
Street, Julian: 11.306
Streit, Clarence K.: 15.53
Strong, L. A. G.: 19.139
Suckow, Ruth: 14.96; 16.61; 16.374
Sullivan, Arthur: 15.55
Sullivan, Mark: 12.298; 14.97; 17.78

Taber, John H.: 12.142
Tandy, Jennette: 11.312
Tarbell, Ida M.: 10.255
Tarkington, Booth: 2.120
Thayer, William Roscoe: 13.151
Thomas, Edward: 17.155
Thomas, Elizabeth Wilkins: 16.188A
Thomas, Helen: 17.155
Thomas, Lowell: 16.126
Thompson, E. N. S.: 1.26
Thompson, Mary Wolfe: 11.130; 15.279
Thompson, Wolfe: 18.203
Thurman, Wallace: 15.157*
Tietjens, Eunice: 11.183
Tomlinson, H. M.: 14.52
Tooker, L. Frank: 11.98
Torrence, Ridgely: 11.310
Towne, Charles Hanson: 13.200
Tracy, Henry Chester: 16.296
Trevelyan, R. C.: 12.39
Trombly, Albert Edmund: 16.189
Trowbridge, Lydia J.: 16.126
Tully, Jim: 11.183
Turner, Ralph E.: 12.74
Tweed, "Boss": 14.101

Unamuno, Miguel de: 12.40; 16.191A

Van Doren, Carl: 11.179; 12.75; 13.117; 15.47; 16.374
Van Doren, Mark: 13.252; 14.104; 17.159
Van Vechten, Carl: 11.100; 11.313; 12.302
Vestal, Stanley: 14.218
Vildrac, Charles: 10.111
Villiers, A. J.: 17.156

Waldron, Webb: 10.206
Waley, Arthur: 12.142
Walrond, Eric: 13.94
Warner, Sylvia Townsend: 13.117; 13.157
Wassermann, Jacob: 13.95; 14.159
Watts, Mrs.: 2.259
Weaver, John V. A.: 12.251
Weaver, Raymond: 12.253
Webb, Mary: 12.223; 15.142; 15.223
Weeks, Raymond: 11.53; 11.173*; 14.266
Weems, Parson: 14.218
Weirick, Bruce: 11.131
Wescott, Glenway: 11.99
West, Rebecca: 13.207
Weston, Mildred: 13.119
Wharton, Edith: 11.313; 12.76; 12.252; 15.49
Wheelock, John Hall: 14.54
Whitcomb, Selden L.: 1.28; 1.135
White, Nelia Gardner: 14.102
White, William Allen: 2.195; 11.178; 11.226
Whitman, Walt: 13.30; 13.153; 17.79
Whitney, Leon F.: 18.203
Whipple, Wayne: 1.319
Wiegler, Paul: 16.190A
Wilde, Oscar: 15.52
Wilder, Thornton: 14.156
Williams, Ben Ames: 14.97; 14.216
Williams, Stanley T.: 12.75
Williamson, Henry: 13.204; 14.155; 15.190; 15.278; 16.189A
Wilson, Edmund: 17.156
Wilson, Margaret: 10.62
Wilson, Woodrow: 11.178
Winkler, John K.: 14.219
Winslow, Thyra Samter: 12.138
Wister, Owen: 15.50
Wolfe, Thomas: 16.125
Wood, Clement: 11.225; 14.216
Woodhull, Victoria Claflin: 15.138
Woodruff, Douglas: 13.155
Wright, Richardson: 14.104
Wyer, Malcolm G.: 1.26
Wyman, Mary Alice: 13.278

Young, Francis Brett: 12.197

Zweig, Arnold: 15.276
Zweig, Stefan: 14.159; 16.190A

Bibliography

THE information contained in this study has been based for the most part on primary materials: volumes one through twenty of *The Midland;* private communications from and private interviews with persons related to the story; manuscript and other materials selected from items in excess of 1,000. The two largest collections of *Midland* materials are in the special collections departments of the libraries at the University of Notre Dame and the University of Iowa. All business records of the journal are in the Notre Dame collection; the original, or a copy of each item used in this study is in the Iowa collection. Also, Mrs. Mildred Mott Wedel, Frank Luther Mott's daughter, has in her possession many items relating to *Midland.*

SECONDARY MATERIALS

BOOKS:

Anderson, Margaret. *My Thirty Years' War.* New York: Horizon Press, 1969.

Ansley, Delight. *First Chronicles.* Doylestown, Pa.: Gardy Printing Co., 1971.

Becker, George J., ed. *Documents of Modern Literary Realism.* Princeton: Princeton University Press, 1963.

Botkin, B. A., ed. *Folk-Say: A Regional Miscellany.* Norman: University of Oklahoma Press, 1930.

Braeman, John, Robert H. Bremner, and David Brody eds. *Change and Continuity in Twentieth Century America: The 1920's.* Columbus: Ohio State University Press, 1968.

Brigham, Johnson, ed. *A Book of Iowa Authors by Iowa Authors.* Des Moines: Iowa State Teachers Association, 1930.

Brooks, Van Wyck. *The Opinions of Oliver Allston.* New York: E. P. Dutton, 1941.

Coffin, Tristram Potter, ed. *Our Living Traditions: An Introduction to American Folklore.* New York: Basic Books, 1968.

Cowan, Louise. *The Fugitive Group: A Literary History.* Baton Rouge: Louisiana State University Press, 1959.

Cowley, Malcolm. *Exile's Return: A Literary Odyssey of the 1920's.* New York: Viking, 1951.

——, ed. *After the Genteel Tradition: American Writers 1910-1930.* Carbondale: Southern Illinois University Press, 1964.

Davidson, Donald. *The Attack on 'Leviathan': Regionalism and Nationalism in the United States.* Chapel Hill, University of North Carolina Press, 1938.

Dolmetsch, Carl R. *The Smart Set: A History and Anthology.* New York: Dial Press, 1966.

Flanagan, John T., ed. *America is West: An Anthology of Middlewestern Life and Literature.* Minneapolis: University of Minnesota Press, 1945.

Frederick, John T. *Druida.* New York: Knopf, 1923.

——. *Green Bush.* New York: Knopf, 1925.

——. *A Handbook of Short Story Writing.* New York: Knopf, 1928.

——. *William Henry Hudson.* New York: Twayne, 1972.

——, ed. *Out of the Midwest.* New York: Knopf, 1944.

——, ed. *Stories from The Midland.* New York: Knopf, 1924.

Garland, Hamlin. *Crumbling Idols: Twelve Essays on Art Dealing Chiefly with Literature, Painting and the Drama,* ed. Jane Johnson. Cambridge: Belknap Press, 1960.

Greenbaum, Leonard. *The Hound and Horn: The History of a Literary Quarterly.* The Hague: Mouton, 1966.

Hemingway, Ernest. *A Moveable Feast.* New York: Scribner, 1964.

Hoffman, Frederick J. *Freudianism and the Literary Mind.* Baton Rouge: Louisiana State University Press, 1957.

——. *The Twenties: American Writing in the Postwar Decade.* New York: Free Press, 1965.

——. Charles Allen, and Carolyn F. Ulrich. *The Little Magazine: A History and a Bibliography.* Princeton: Princeton University Press, 1946.

Hofstadter, Richard. *The Age of Reform: from Bryan to FDR.* New York: Knopf, 1955.

Howells, William Dean. *Criticism and Fiction and Other Essays,* ed. Clara M. Kirk and Rudolph Kirk. New York: New York University Press, 1959.

Jensen, Merrill, ed. *Regionalism in America.* Madison: University of Wisconsin Press, 1951.

Jones, Howard Mumford. *The Theory of American Literature.* Ithaca: Cornell University Press, 1965.

Joost, Nicholas. *Years of Transition: The Dial 1912-1920.* Barre, Mass.: Barre Publishers, 1967.

Lee, Robert Edson. *From West to East: Studies in the Literature of the American West*. Urbana: University of Illinois Press, 1966.

Macy, John. *The Spirit of American Literature*. Garden City, N. Y.: Doubleday, Page, 1913.

Marshall, Max L. *"Frank Luther Mott: Journalism Educator."* Ph.D. dissertation, University of Missouri, 1968.

May, Henry F. *The End of American Innocence: A Study of the First Years of our Own Time, 1912-1917*. New York: Knopf, 1959.

McWilliams, Carey. *The New Regionalism in American Literature*. Seattle: University of Washington Book Store, 1930.

Meyer, Roy Willard. *The Middle Western Farm Novel in the Twentieth Century*. Lincoln: University of Nebraska Press, 1965.

Monroe, Harriet. *A Poet's Life: Seventy Years in a Changing World*. New York: Macmillan, 1938.

Mott, Frank Luther. *A History of American Magazines: 1885-1905*. Cambridge: Belknap Press, 1957.

———. *A History of American Magazines: 1905-1930*. Cambridge: Belknap Press, 1968.

———. *Time Enough: Essays in Autobiography*. Chapel Hill: University of North Carolina Press, 1962.

O'Brien, Edward J. *The Advance of the American Short Story*. New York: Dodd, Mead, 1923.

———. *The Dance of the Machines: The American Short Story and the Industrial Age*. New York: Macaulay, 1929.

———, ed. *The Best Short Stories of 1915 and the Yearbook of the American Short Story*. Boston: Small, Maynard, 1916.

———, ed. *The Best Short Stories of 1930 and the Yearbook of the American Short Story*. New York: Dodd, Mead, 1930.

Odum, Howard W., and Harry Estill Moore. *American Regionalism: A Cultural-Historical Approach to National Integration*. New York: Henry Holt, 1938.

Peterson, Theodore B. *Magazines in the Twentieth Century*. Urbana: University of Illinois Press, 1964.

Rideout, Walter B. *The Radical Novel in the United States, 1900-1954*. Cambridge: Harvard University Press, 1956.

Royce, Josiah. *Race Questions, Provincialism, and Other American Problems*. New York: Macmillan, 1908.

Sacks, Claire. *"The Seven Arts Critics: A Study of Cultural Nationalism in America, 1910-1930."* Ph.D. dissertation, University of Wisconsin, 1955.

Singleton, Marvin K. *H. L. Mencken and the American Mercury Adventure*. Durham: Duke University Press, 1962.

Stewart, Paul R. *The Prairie Schooner Story*. Lincoln: University of Nebraska Press, 1955.

Tebbel, John. *The American Magazine: A Compact History*. New York: Hawthorne Books, 1969.

Trippet, Mary Maud. "A History of *The Southwest Review:* Toward an Understanding of Regionalism." Ph.D. dissertation, University of Illinois, 1966.

Turner, Frederick Jackson. *The Frontier in American History*. New York: Henry Holt, 1920.

Turner, Susan J. *A History of The Freeman: Literary Landmark of the Early Twenties*. New York: Columbia University Press, 1963.

Twelve Southerners. *I'll Take My Stand: The South and the Agrarian Tradition*. New York: Harper and Brothers, 1930.

Wasserstrom, William. *The Time of the Dial*. New York: Syracuse University Press, 1963.

Whittemore, Reed. *Little Magazines*. Minneapolis: University of Minnesota Press, 1963.

Wolseley, Roland E. *Understanding Magazines*. Ames: Iowa State University Press, 1965.

Wood, James Playsted. *Magazines in the United States*. New York: Ronald Press, 1956.

Wright, Austin R. *The American Short Story in the Twenties*. Chicago: University of Chicago Press, 1961.

ARTICLES:

Anon. "The Boom in Regionalism." *Saturday Review of Literature* 10 (7 April 1934):606.

Austin, Mary. "Regionalism in American Fiction." *English Journal* 21 (February 1931):97-106.

Baker, Joseph E. "Four Arguments for Regionalism." *Saturday Review of Literature* 15 (28 November 1936):3-4, 14.

Beath, Paul Robert. "The Fallacies of Regionalism." *Saturday Review of Literature* 15 (28 November 1936):3-4, 14, 16.

Cowley, Malcolm. "Magazine Business: 1910-1946." *New Republic* 115 (21 October 1946):5, 35.

Flanagan, John T. "Some Midwestern Literary Magazines." *Papers on Language and Literature* 3 (Summer 1967):237-53.

Frederick, John T. "Culture of Communities." *Community Life in a Democracy*, ed. F. C. Bingham. Chicago: National Council of Parents and Teachers, 1942.

—— "The Farm in Iowa Fiction." *Palimpsest* 32 (March 1957): 121-52.

———. "Literary Evening — Iowa Style." *The Borzoi 1925.* New York: Knopf, 1925.

———. "The Meaning of Literature in America Today." *What America Stands For,* ed. I. Kertesz and M. A. Fitzsimons. South Bend: University of Notre Dame Press, 1959.

———. "Ruth Suckow and the Middle Western Literary Movement." *English Journal* 20 (January 1931):1-8.

———. "The Younger School." *Palimpsest* 11 (February 1930):78-86.

Hartley, Lois T. "The Midland." *Iowa Journal of History* 47 (October 1949):325-44.

McLeod, Norman, *et al.* "Regionalism: A Symposium." *Sewanee Review* 39 (October-December 1931):456-83.

Merriam, Howard G. "Expression of Northwest Life." *New Mexico Quarterly* 6 (May 1934):127-32.

Mott, Frank Luther. "Iowa Literary Magazines." *Palimpsest* 11 (February 1930):87-94.

———. "The Midland." *Palimpsest* 43 (March 1962):133-44.

Pound, Ezra. "Small Magazines." *English Journal* 19 (November 1930): 689-704.

Ransom, John Crowe. "The Aesthetics of Regionalism." *American Review* 2 (January 1934):290-310.

Stegner, Wallace. "The Trail of the Hawkeye: Literature Where the Tall Corn Grows." *Saturday Review of Literature* 18 (30 July 1938): 1, 3-4, 16-17.

Suckow, Ruth. "Middle Western Literature." *English Journal* 21 (March 1932):175-82.

Tate, Allen. "Regionalism and Sectionalism." *New Republic* 69 (23 December 1931):158-59.

Troy, William. "The Story of the Little Magazines: The Revolt in the Desert." *Bookman* 70 (January 1930):476-81.

———. "The Story of the Little Magazines: Making No Compromise with the Public Taste." *Bookman* 70 (February 1930):657-63.

Warren, Robert Penn. "Some Don'ts for Literary Regionalists." *American Review* 8 (December 1936);142-50.

Wright, Louella M. "The Midland Monthly." *Iowa Journal of History and Politics* 45 (January 1947):3-61.

Milton M. Reigelman, who was born in Washington, D.C., received an A.B. in philosophy from the College of William and Mary and worked for *The Washington Post* before receiving a Masters of Communication from the University of Pennsylvania. While teaching at The University of Iowa, he received an M.A. and a Ph.D. in English. He now teaches English and American literature at Centre College of Kentucky in Danville.